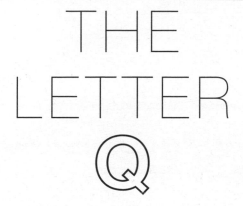

# THE
# LETTER
# Q

Queer Writers' Notes to Their Younger Selves

*Edited by Sarah Moon*
*with Contributing Editor James Lecesne*

SCHOLASTIC INC.

No part of this publication may be reproduced, stored in a retrieval system, or transmitted in any form or by any means, electronic, mechanical, photocopying, recording, or otherwise, without written permission of the publisher. For information regarding permission, write to Scholastic Inc., Attention: Permissions Department, 557 Broadway, New York, NY 10012.

ISBN 978-0-545-39933-3

Arthur A. Levine Books hardcover edition designed by Kristina Iulo, published by Arthur A. Levine Books, an imprint of Scholastic Inc., May 2012.

12 11 10 9 8 7 6 5 4 3 2 1    14 15 16 17 18 19 /0

Printed in the U.S.A.  40

First paperback printing, May 2014

The text type was set in Lino Letter Roman.

Book design by Kristina Iulo

*FOR MS. FREYDA ROSE,*
*MY FIRST-GRADE TEACHER,*
*WHO GUIDES ME STILL.*
*— SM*

*FOR ANYONE WHO THOUGHT*
*THEY COULDN'T MAKE IT.*
*AND THEN DID.*
*— JL*

# TABLE OF CONTENTS

# HEY

Thanks for reading. We hope you like this book.

When I (Sarah) was a kid, I was really lucky and really unlucky. Unlucky because I lived in the middle of nowhere and was an enormous homosexual; I knew it, my friends knew it, everyone knew it. Long before I came out to myself or to anyone else, people were calling me a dyke or a boy in school every day; they spit on me and threw eggs at my house. Not such great luck.

Luckily, though, I found myself surrounded by adults who'd been through what I'd been through and lived to tell the tale. They weren't like a lot of people I knew; they weren't hypocritical, or scared, or unbelievably boring. They were these smart, queer, caring people who decided to help me. They told me stories. They wrote me letters. I folded them up and carried them with me to school every day. In the beginning of tenth grade, things started getting a lot worse. I was sick of it. I started shouting back at the people who called me names. Not exactly the path of least resistance. My friends started to feel like hanging out with me was pretty risky. I started eating lunch in the bathroom. Then, I found the back stairwell where it was quiet and there was a window. I'd sit on the stairs with my french-fry lunch (very clever revenge on health-food-nut parents, I thought), and I'd take out the right letter for whatever was going on that day. When the school ruled against the Gay-Straight Alliance and it became clear to me that I would be spending much of the year in the principal's office, or one kid had followed me around calling me a dyke all morning and I just couldn't imagine facing the rest of my day, I would take out the one that said, *This is the life of an activist in a small town. It is not permanent, but it is difficult. I swear to you, you will not be sixteen forever.* When I was crushing on straight girl after straight girl after straight girl, I got some hard-learned advice: *First of all, the straight ones are no fun. Second of all, they will break your heart. I settled for them too, back in the day. But the good stuff is worth waiting for.* When I finally found a gay girl to date, I read the one that came with instructions: *Ask her out, honey! Call her up and take her to the movies. Halfway through, hold her hand.* When we broke up (after three weeks) it was: *The first one hurts the worst. It's okay to hug pillows and cry until you can deal.* When I started to hurt myself my junior year, the directions were clear: *You need to talk to your mama.* And there was one that I read every day, one that saw straight through me, that said, *You are not a terrible person, baby. You are terrified and angry. The more you talk, the more it'll lessen. I promise you. Now promise me.* I had no idea how she knew. I promised.

So, what does someone who hated school grow up to be? A teacher, of course. That's how I know that while a lot has changed since I was a teenager, a lot hasn't. I've taught in cities and suburbs, public and private, even a jail, and they all have one thing in common — they're full of kids who are trying to make their ways through moments of fear, insecurity, doubt, despair, confusion, hilarity, openheartedness, giddiness, and overwhelming joy. Just like all of us.

It didn't seem quite fair to me that I should have been the only teenager to get wonderful letters to carry around with her. The first person I asked to write a letter for this book was James Lecesne, founder of The Trevor Project, an organization dedicated to preventing LGBTQ teen suicide. You can get in touch with them anytime, day or night; check the back pages of this book for more information. Together, James and I asked writers we trusted, liked, admired, and made us laugh to write letters telling their younger selves what they could do to make their lives a little better, a little lighter. In turn, they asked their writer friends to do the same, and we have this book. The letters we got back are funny, kind, and honest, like the best sort of people. Mostly, though, they are very good company.

We hope they help.


All our love,


*Sarah and James*

# AMY BLOOM

*Dear Amy,*

There's all sorts of good news from here in the future: You really will get the hang of high heels (you will not go through life feeling like a soft-boiled egg on stilts) and then you will have a big fat epiphany and choose not to do that to your feet (except for very special occasions). You will not be waitressing into middle age. (You could but you won't have to.) Your abysmal performance in all things mathematic won't really matter (computers and calculators and common sense will fill in your ginormous educational gaps).

Please, love your eighteen-year-old body because it's not gonna get better than that. (Better at tennis and the foxtrot, yes — more perfect, no.)

So let's talk about everything your dear body can do, will do, and does.

Most of the sensible adults you know will say — if they say anything at all — bad things about one-night stands. I'm not so sure. They are people — certain types, certain experiences — that you might not want to miss out on. Be careful, be smart (you know what this means: Do not have sex with anyone if you're not capable of driving yourself home; use condoms, always, always; no sketchy drugs from sketchy guys, and good luck knowing when to bail). Once is sometimes enough and once is sometimes necessary. If you hadn't cuddled up in nothing but your panties to that cute girl from the other high school — after a night of rock and roll and her mother's Tia Maria — you might not have known that you liked girls too. And that would have been a shame. It's true, you don't know anyone just like you, but they're out there. And, furthermore, what strikes you as an unusual but not disturbing penchant is going to make your life bigger and better, as well as bumpier. It will probably help you become the very good couples therapist that you become. (Did I mention this? You become a shrink and then a writer. I know — you really did think you'd be waitressing at O'Malley's into your fifties.) When the men say their wives nag them to death, you sympathize, 'cause you've had girlfriends. When the wives say that they wouldn't nag if the knucklehead just listened the first time, you sympathize, 'cause you've had boyfriends.

I know you worry that you don't have enough sticking power, that when you get fed up, you leave, and not too many people get a whole three strikes. You worry that you can't stay the course of things that matter. I know you worry that your distant father and anxious mother have produced in you . . . mostly a desire to get out of Dodge at the first signs of disappointment. You will get better at this, although you do — sorry to tell you — continue to struggle. You will discover that your mother's warmth and your father's unshakable and baseless confidence in you, although it takes the form of no intervention and not much interest, combine to make you a loving, weirdly confident person. Could be worse.

You will find yourself with a best friend (thirty years and counting), a beloved sister (yes, you start talking to each other, finally), three amazing children who have many of your best qualities and only some of your faults, and the kind of spouse (as it turns out, a husband) you hoped for and thought you'd never find.

Much love to you, self.

*Amy*

# MICHAEL CUNNINGHAM

*Dear Michael,*

Worry less. Use what the world has given you.
That's all I've got to tell you, really.

I can, however, elaborate a bit.

You'll get to be a writer, even though I know that right now, it seems as if publishing is Jupiter, and you're trying to get there using only the tools you have around the house. Even though the rejection slips seem to arrive the day after you've sent your stories to a magazine. I know you'll keep writing — you're nothing if not determined. But try to entertain a lower degree of panic as you do.

And, in your writing, do stop trying to conform.

I know you all too well. I know that you're going to spend years writing the stories you think readers want to read: relatively conventional stories about, yes, straight people. I wish it wasn't too late to talk you out of that. I know how desperate you feel; how convinced you are that anyone who hasn't made it by his mid-twenties has been left munching the dust as the parade marches on. You've started writing stories at the age of fourteen and, yes, it seems they're a little too "arty," too plotless and contemplative, for your high school literary magazine (which favors tales of surfing, dating, and triumph over vice). Later on you'll be slinging cocktails in various Southern California gay bars, and, finding that your stories are *still* too "arty" for larger magazines, you'll imagine your future self as the oldest living bartender, all red-faced and snaggle-toothed, with wiry hairs sprouting from unfortunate places, telling anyone who'll listen that you're really a writer, and are just waiting for that first big break.

With each rejection slip, that future feels more horrifyingly likely.

And now, here comes the big surprise.

As you're nearing thirty, you'll say, screw it, maybe I'll never be recognized, but I still want to write. It's the only thing I've ever wanted to do. So I'm going to start writing about the people who matter most to me, the people I know best. I'm going to stop trying to court the *New Yorker* with tales of adultery and divorce in Connecticut. I'm going to write about gay people. I can live with the idea that no one will ever publish me. When I'm the oldest living bartender, I'll try to keep those errant hairs plucked.

And that's when your writing career will take off. Try to believe me.

After ten years of writing the stories you think editors will want to edit and readers to read, you'll learn that you were mistaken. What editors want to edit and readers want to read is fiction that's passionate, urgent, and true. It doesn't matter to them if the characters are gay or straight.

I told you it was a big surprise.

The *New Yorker* (aka the planet Jupiter) will buy the first story you send them that *isn't* some trumped-up tale of adultery and divorce in Connecticut. As it'll turn out, they're tired of those stories too. They see dozens of them every day. A story by an obstreperous and unapologetic gay man, about obstreperous and unapologetic gay men, is a rarer bird there.

When that story appears in the *New Yorker*, everything will change. It'll stand out in ways that the more conventional *New Yorker* stories don't. Editors who've read this particular oddity in those rather staid pages will start calling. You'll be on your way.

I'd be lying if I said it was going to be easy or fun all the time.

Will some people, critics prominent among them, dismiss you as a niche writer, at first? Yes. Will Terry Gross, on NPR, want to talk to you about your sexuality instead of your book? Uh-huh.

Will your parents, who were traumatized enough when you came out to them, be re-traumatized when you become a public gay person? Will they fret over the fact that you're not only out to them, you are now out to the entire nation of Japan? You can count on it.

Don't waver, though. Literature is moved forward by writers who insist on their own particularities, and even their peculiarities. Critics don't matter, not over the long haul. Parents get over it (though not necessarily as quickly as you might like them to).

By the time you're in your fifties, you'll be seen as a writer first, and as a gay writer second. You'll get uncountable letters from readers who've been moved by your books, and you will treasure especially the letters from gay men and lesbians who thank you for telling stories that include them.

One more thing.

I should tell you that I recently received a letter like this from myself at the age of eighty-five. He told me essentially the same thing. Worry less. Love being exactly who and what you are, which, at present, is a middle-aged writer who's come to question the importance of novels in the larger scheme of things. Don't fret about aging, don't worry about your career, just do what you were meant to do.

As he tells me, I'm only fifty-eight. Lap it up, he says. When I'm eighty-five, I'll look back and wonder why I worried the way I did.

So lap it up, young'un. Worry less. Have faith in the fact that your sexual identity, which sometimes seems to you like an impediment, is one of your greatest gifts.

And oh, don't worry about the time you tipsily confess your passion to your best friend, and he never speaks to you again. I know it seems like a huge trauma right now. But you know what? As a few more years pass, you won't miss him. You'll barely even notice he's gone.


Love,


*Michael*

# JULIE ANNE PETERS

*Dear Julie at 16,*

Sitting on that picnic table in Woodbury Park at midnight, hugging your knees and bawling your eyes out, wishing someone would come along and murder you because whatever method they chose would hurt less than the pain you were feeling at being dumped by him — the actual, physical ache inside, as if your heart had been crushed, or cleaved in two and you were bleeding internally, and you knew you'd never heal or be loved again with the same intensity and raw emotion. The worst part was that you'd loved with your whole self; you'd given him your most precious virtue. Irretrievable. Lost forever. And the funny part, if any of it was funny, was that you didn't blame him. You were unlovable. You were defective. You weren't good enough for anyone to desire in the way you needed so desperately to be wanted and loved.

I wish there was a time machine because I would've jumped aboard and set the controls to that park. I'd have held you tight and told you that it wasn't you; that in a few short years you'd meet the love of your life, and it would shock you to know who it'd turn out to be.

They say life is lived backward as much as forward, and it's easy to see now that your earliest leanings were for girls. Your relationships with your friends were always tight, solid. You could trust them completely, and you did. I know you remember Lea from that summer camp at Flying G Ranch when you were twelve. You and Lea instantly connected. She made you laugh. You made her laugh. You giggled long into the night until your other cabinmates complained and the camp counselors told you to shut it down. Whenever you weren't assigned to be on the same team for camp activities, you were totally bummed. But then you'd be back together later, hugging, or linking arms and talking and laughing.

You cried for a week when camp ended. It wasn't over the runny oatmeal for breakfast or the s'mores or the hokey ghost stories told around the campfire. (You and Lea giggled your way through those too.) After camp, you promised to write, and you might have for a while, but then you lost track of her, or she forgot, and your life went on.

When your parents divorced, and you moved to North High in Denver, there she was! You don't know if, in the hall the first time your eyes met and held, she recognized you or not, but you definitely knew her. Of course, she was with her friends and you were too shy to just go up and say, "Hi, Lea. Remember me from Flying G?" Because what if she didn't?

You made your own friends — you've always made girl friends

easily — and Lea wasn't one of them. She had her own clique. But then you signed up for this Outward Bound raft trip for two weeks and it was as if destiny was changing the course of a river because she signed up too. You were even assigned to the same raft. Raft #5.

The trip was a rerun of Girl Scout camp, a thousand times over. Inseparable. Laughing and talking until only the stars were awake. Giggling at nothing and everything. Just feeling sort of goofy in love. You'd never felt such a strong bond with any other person, including him.

After the trip, you expected to be "joined at the hip," as they say. And you tried. Lea had a scooter and took you out on joyrides. You hung out for a while, but her friends weren't your friends, and vice versa, and eventually you both gravitated back to before Raft #5. Even if you had recognized that the feelings went beyond friendship, this was the 1960s. Girls didn't do that kind of thing.

You know now you had romantic feelings for other girls in your life. There was Nancy and Cathy and Becky. But it wasn't until college that you came out to yourself. You didn't even have a word for it. Lesbian. Even now it makes you cringe a little. You prefer gay. It makes you happy, that word, and all you ever wanted was to be happy. Free of pain and suffering. Secure in a relationship.

In that time machine, I'd bring back a crystal ball and hold it up to you. "See that girl?" I'd say. "The one in the plaid pants who swags with pride like she owns the planet? That's Sherri. You're going to hook up with her in five years and spend the rest of your lives together." The odds of that happening to anyone are so slim, and you were still hurting from him, and I might have had to con-vince you. But I'd say, "Yep. He's not The One. She is."

Then I would've told you to get the hell out of that park in the middle of the night before you got murdered.

Love,

*Julie Now*

# Jacqueline Woodson

*Dear Mandy,*

I call you this because I know at twelve, this is what you longed for people to call you. You listened to the Barry Manilow song daily and deduced that since your middle name is Amanda, he was writing that song for you. You knew all the words and pictured yourself in each scene of it:

*Well, you came and you gave without taking. But I sent you away. . . .*

But you haven't sent anyone away. It confuses you that this song saddens you and touches you so. You don't know just yet that this sadness is your growing understanding that this is the world you're walking into — a world where, for a long time, you will feel an un-belonging, a sense that people are sending you away from them. And I guess, in a way they are. Your best friend is still your best friend. You see each other every single day and it's hard to be apart. But there is an apartness now. Maria will stay in your life. She'll move to Florida with Sam, who neither of you know yet but who you will introduce her to. They'll have three beautiful daughters and the oldest will eventually move back to the city and become a part of your life. But as I write this, you are realizing that you and Maria are very different. Somewhere deep, you know you will never marry. Not the way the rest of the world around you seems to do it. You don't yet have a name for who you're becoming because in your small world of Madison Street, you don't know what this thing is yet. You see Maria's Auntie Alma. You love her — her huge Afro, her pretty dark eyes. And you love Green Eyes too — the woman Alma shows up with when she comes to visit. Green Eyes is beautiful, soft-spoken, and delicate as dust. You feel clumsy around Green Eyes. And years later, you'll remember that's the only name you had for her. But you have some strange connection to these two women that you don't yet understand. Alma scares you — she is tall and thin and dresses like a man. Your mother calls her a *bulldagger* and this word alone — when said the way your mother says it — makes you afraid to get too close to Alma. You think, *That isn't me.* You are already thinking, *That isn't me.* Because somewhere deep, you know that it is. That you are becoming . . . And your becoming will frighten a lot of people. You don't understand yet why your mother doesn't call Green Eyes a bulldagger. Doesn't say it with the same disdain. You are not concerned with pleasing your mother. You just don't want to piss her off. You walk lightly through this confusing adolescence. On Friday nights, your mother lets you spend the night at Maria's. Some Fridays, when you say Let's play Alma and Green Eyes, Maria says yes. And these are the most wonderful

Fridays — a whole night of being who you are becoming. But soon Maria will say No more of that. We need to find boyfriends. Maybe you are thirteen by then. Maybe twelve and a half. You will try to forget this moment. And for a long time, it will remain in some murky place in your memory — half-forgotten but painful still.

Mandy? I want to tell you, it gets better. There is a whole world of women like you out here. They are amazing! They are mothers and doctors and lawyers and writers and actors and electricians and builders and thinkers and doers. They are funny and thoughtful and caring. Some wear their love proudly, speak out loud about it, declare it as fiercely as they once hid it. Others are shier, quieter, maybe still, a little bit afraid. Maybe still, trying to figure out exactly who they are becoming. And like you, right now, they're still girls — meaning — one day, you will find each other and you will build communities and you will change the world.

But right now, I want you to just take one step — away from Madison Street. Off the block, around the corner, onto the L train, into Manhattan — just go somewhere! And look into the faces of other people. The world is big — and there is so much love in it. I promise you — you will find it. It is already, as I write this, moving toward you.

Love,

*Jacqueline Woodson*

# EILEEN MYLES

*Dear Eileen,*

I saw you standing there today in the cafeteria looking quite frozen and I wanted to tell you that we in the future understand your insides and are here now to tell you that miraculously you will be okay, um, even by the time you are in your twenties, which I know seems like quite a ways off. I promise you won't always be standing there stuck in your horrible Catholic school all your life, feeling like if you sit with your friends there will only be more abuse unless you agree to be funny and mock yourself all the time. And all the time knowing the cruelty will come again as soon as Janet has her next horrible idea. Notice that you and Janet bond around one thing — self-mockery — and so at school dances the two of you go out of your way to do the most obscene ludicrous moves to let everyone know that you think THEY are gross and the only way it can be expressed is by becoming gross yourselves. You and Janet take part in your mutual pain in these dances and from where I sit I can't say for sure that Janet was also a lesbian — but whatever she is or was she just didn't have the good fortune you ultimately do have to find yourself in a culture that HAS room for you to explore who you might be outside of the Arlington Catholic High School bastion of mean suburban conventionality. Ugh. Know that WE in the future all hate that place. Know that when you are older no one from there will still even care that you are now a writer and a poet and sometimes most important, a lesbian. They are that dumb. In fact in the future your selfhood will only continue to weird them out. But by then you'll have found a world of people even weirder than you, just better than the past, simply loving, open and confident, angry sometimes but welcoming. You'll meet people all over the world in person and through your work who will make it abundantly clear that what sails through your mind delights them, and the adventure of that encounter will bring you love and friendship and even some success but mostly it will bring you this crazy smiling part of yourself that will look back at you at thirteen or fifteen and even twelve (Hi!) and say honestly, You will be blown away by who you will grow up into. So I would like to urge you to lighten up on the self-mockery and let Janet find someone else to do the ugly dancing with because you might just want to dance — not so anyone else sees you and gets the twisted message of turned inside-out anger and fear, but so YOU can feel the music and be part of the whole room swaying and bouncing inside and out and not be having to send a message at all to anyone. Just dance, get out there and swim. 'Cause right now you are in the dancing years of your life and if you like dancing at all — and I know you do — you should be doing it for yourself, feverishly and exhaustively. Same with singing. You know those mock-up girl bands you do for the high school talent shows. You love doing that and should not just do mock-ups. Girls can do bands. You know those drums you saw one day gleaming in the basement of one of those boys in Lexington. You wanted to sit down and play even though you don't know how. You should do it. Don't be afraid of making a fool of yourself, do what you want. All those things you are good at: drawing and painting, writing funny shit that everyone in school likes you to read out loud in class, those songs you write for the girl band, the plays you write so you won't flunk history. That is art. It's the work you will be doing for the rest of your life so be proud of these things that are easy for you. If something is easy for you, it means that big parts of you are being used and you should begin to do that thing with your eyes open and do it until it gets hard. Move something around and it will get easy again. You should look for other kids who are into what you are into and stick with them. The kids who are mean to you are a waste of time. Don't let them talk you into quitting ballet class because it's "queer." Do you know what queer means? Obviously you are secretly a boy in a way that is turning you inside out, which is part of why you are standing there stuck in the cafeteria today, but you know — so many people are mixes of male and female — and despite the fact of your secret boy, you probably also have secret female parts you don't even know about yet. Gender is the great mystery of the world (like love) and all the ways you let yourself be terrorized by your friends who think your discomfort, your tomboyishness, your awkward energy is something you should be shamed for is a giant waste of time. They are suffering and they have YOU to pick on. If you just walk away from them and remain the mystery you are, the mystery will draw other kinds of people to you. Some you already know, some you will meet in a few years. By the way, most of the people in your family are queer and that's part of the silence you feel around the house and part of the creepiness you feel in your family from one person to the next. Everyone's afraid of what queer means and you will be the first to find out. You can be the first person in your family who lived frankly. So don't give up. Write in your diary, go where it's warm, i.e., toward people who act like they like you, and bear in mind that some of them will also seem weird. Pay attention to how the person FEELS when you spend time with them, not how you will look when you show up with them in your world. The world you are in today is really small. Think of the kids you meet on the bus to Harvard Square. Think of how good it feels to be one of them, getting out of town to go hear music. Do not, above all, let your family ever convince you to stay home when it's time to go. That thing in you that feels like you are ready to leave them — for college or after or even just at a family party — feeling trapped there — always know that you have the right to go. Just as you have the right to be yourself here (and everywhere). The fact that you might not have the means to go AT THIS MOMENT is hard but know that you are ready and that your destiny is to live your life, not theirs, and though it hurts to leave home you will always find a bigger better one that is your own. The world is open to you, unbelievably. You are great, funny, beautiful, and completely wild. And you are already big enough and strong enough and wise enough to make a go in it and become part of its story. So start talking now. Meet yourself. Meet the people. And if they can't listen to you and can't hold your attention, then go talk to someone else. And someone else again. You'll find the right ones. We of the future are waiting for you to make us laugh at the secrets you've been holding inside for so long. It's your joy and we urge you to not be selfish and keep it all to yourself. Your joy, like a dog, wants to go for a walk. And by the way, in the future you will have many dogs, so don't regret that part of your past. The painful unanimalness of your childhood and teens. Dogs are in your future. Great ones — who are waiting to meet you — so go ahead. Say hello, move toward them. Welcome! WOOF!

*Eileen*

# DAVID LEVITHAN

*Dear David in Eighth Grade,*

I hate to say it, but I think you owe Mr. Jones an apology.

Not for being an uninspiring teacher. He is a deeply uninspiring teacher. But, to be fair, it's hard to imagine anyone inspiring you in eighth-grade Earth Science. "Schist" puns aside, there's not much in this class for you to latch on to.

So, yes, you're bored. Monumentally bored. To the degree that you spend much of the period writing notes or watching the patterns of the dandruff that falls onto the black table-desk. I get it.

But that's not really a reason to be mean.

I'm not talking about the harmless jokes. The time he showed a slide of a girl putting her tongue to a piece of quartz to check its taste, and you yelled out, "It's *Romancing the Stone!*" Priceless. But the way you slagged him for being gay? Oh, there's a price for that one.

I don't even remember how it started. He pissed you off in some way. Maybe by being so boring. Maybe by not leaving you alone to be bored. But suddenly you unpacked the insult. He was wearing a pale pink sweater and you started joking that he was gay. And that really got to him.

Nowadays, we have these things called "teachable moments," and if Mr. Jones had been a certain kind of educator, he might have defused your insult by telling you how inconsequential it was, and that if he was in fact gay, it wouldn't matter. But of course, you're living twenty-five years ago, and Mr. Jones isn't a certain kind of educator, so instead of telling you it would be okay if he were gay (although he isn't), he starts to drop references to his girlfriend all over his class. Seriously, every time he can fit in a mention of it, he does. ("My girlfriend and I were looking at cumulus clouds the other day," etc.) You sense that you're winning, so you keep calling out his sham, doubting his girlfriend's existence. You think he doth protest too much. People think this is hysterical. You make them laugh. A lot. And that feels good.

The weird thing is, you're not motivated by homophobia. You don't, to my memory, call anyone else gay as an insult. Ever. But with Mr. Jones, you sense that this is the one thing that will make him the most uncomfortable — it's the shining arrow in your arsenal, and you use it over and over again. Until eventually it gets boring too, and you go back to your dandruff.

I have no idea if there's such a thing as retroactive gaydar, but I'm pretty certain now that Mr. Jones is not, in fact, gay. And you, indeed, are.

I'm still not entirely sure whether I use the word *irony* correctly, but I believe there's something exquisitely ironic about making fun of your non-gay teacher for being gay, and then going home and listening to Barbra Streisand's *Broadway Album* over and over again.

I know many gay people now who honed their caustic wit as a defense mechanism — this particular rapier was the best thing in their own arsenals, so they made sure it was sharp as possible, and sometimes they went in for the kill. Hell, sometimes they still do.

Don't fall into this trap. It doesn't make you safe. It only makes you mean.

Right now, there's a lot of talk about bullying. And I think of you every time the issue comes up. Because, I'll be honest, a lot of the time bullying is presented as an either/or thing: either you're bullied or you're a bully. The gay kid is the victim. The bully is the Bad Guy.

But that isn't your experience, is it?

Because you're both a bully *and* bullied. You attack — not with your fists, but with your words. And you're attacked. Never with fists, but there is something about you that inexplicably makes assholes want to spit on you. Such a childish gesture, but man, it sinks in.

The thing is? What you do to Mr. Jones — or the other cutdowns you make about what classmates are wearing, or how stupid other kids are — is not justified by what you yourself are going through. You're both innocent and guilty. You are a sweet, intelligent guy that I'm proud of now, and you're also an occasional asshole that I still can't believe I was.

The good news is that I don't really have to tell you that

meanness is wrong; you'll figure it out yourself, soon. And I don't really have to tell you that you're gay; you'll figure that one out as well. The taunts you get in high school — all those times you're called gay as an insult, all the stupid spitting that comes with it — won't really slow you down, because by then you'll have a sense of context about the world, and you'll know that you lead a pretty charmed life.

I'm happy to be able to tell you that at age thirty-eight, you're not going to want to go back and change many things about your life. You'll realize the successes and the failures are inextricably linked, and you wouldn't sacrifice any of the parts because that would alter the whole, which is still pretty charmed.

That said, the only times you'll want to change are the times you reached into that arsenal and used the weapons you had at your disposal. The way to deal with bullies isn't to condemn them, it's to understand them. In your case, the boys who spit on you will end up being real fuck-ups, miserable and desperate in their own ways. Some will have seen something in you that they didn't want to recognize in themselves, and will be attacking that. Others will be so messed up on drugs, loneliness, or the mix of the two that they won't even appreciate what they're doing. Others are simply, inexcusably mean, and wear that meanness as an extension of the privileges life has given them.

And then there will be the bullies like you. Smart kids doing stupid things, in love with the power that their voices can have. Sometimes this is the only power that they possess, and I have sympathy for that. But with you, there are other ways to be clever, other ways to get attention. Eventually you'll find them. Just not in eighth grade.

I have a scary feeling that Mr. Jones was younger then than I am now. I know it's a stretch to ask you to imagine the point of view of an Earth Science teacher, but eventually such things are possible. And you'll see: Make all the jokes you want. Make people laugh. But don't do it at someone else's expense. It gives you a rush, to be the star for a moment, to have your words hit so hard. But that rush only leads you to a place you don't need to be.

Sincerely,

*David Now*

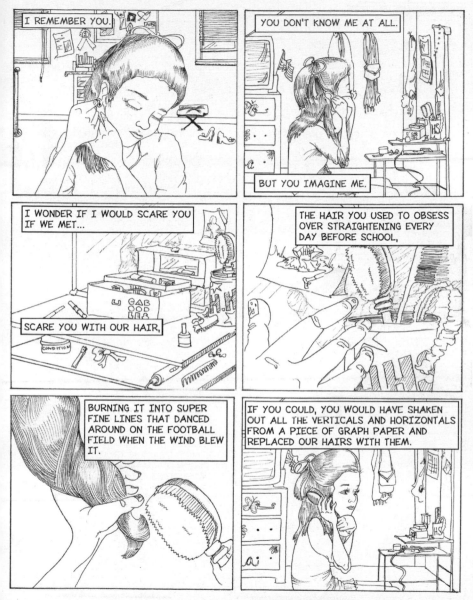

THE IRONY OF OUR LOCATION WAS LOST ON YOU,

BUT THE IMPORTANCE OF YOUR QUIETEST THOUGHTS WERE NOT.

YOU SAID TO OURSELF:

THERE IS THE DISTINCT POSSIBILITY THAT I LIKE GIRLS...

...BUT I CAN'T LIVE HERE AND BE BIRACIAL AND BE QUEER...

YOU LET THE THOUGHT COME TO US THAT ONE TIME, AND THEN YOU NEVER THOUGHT ABOUT IT AGAIN.

YOU BURIED THESE SECRETS DEEP IN THE LINES OF YOUR DIARY,

DISGUISED AS OBSESSIONS OVER BOYS WHO LIKED YOU BUT HATED YOUR SKIN,

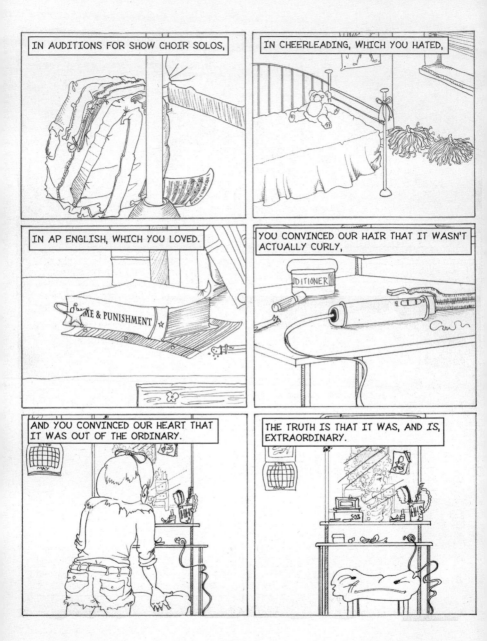

IN AUDITIONS FOR SHOW CHOIR SOLOS,

IN CHEERLEADING, WHICH YOU HATED,

IN AP ENGLISH, WHICH YOU LOVED.

YOU CONVINCED OUR HAIR THAT IT WASN'T ACTUALLY CURLY,

AND YOU CONVINCED OUR HEART THAT IT WAS OUT OF THE ORDINARY.

THE TRUTH IS THAT IT WAS, AND *IS*, EXTRAORDINARY.

32

# RAKESH SATYAL

*Dear Rakesh,*

Ｓee — someone *can* spell your name correctly. Because, well, that someone is you.

This is you, about twenty years in the future. No, I did not somehow commandeer Marty McFly's DeLorean, and no, I can't get you a kiss from Michael J. Fox either. I *can* get you a signed copy of his eventual memoir, *Always Looking Up*, but I know that's not as cool as the fortune-making almanac from *Back to the Future Part II*. I did, however, buy *Always Looking Up* off eBay. I won't go into all the specifics of what that means, but if you ever wondered what will happen down the line to all of those Happy Meal toys that you've been collecting, just know that eBay will be heavily involved in their fate.

First, the bad news: You're balding. The good news is that you have a finely shaped head. Pull out those old baby pictures and you'll have a sense of what to expect. And believe it or not, you still have that rosy glow on your cheeks (you're still brown, though, so don't freak out). Some other good news: You're gay.

What — that doesn't sound good? Well, it's certainly not *news* to you, Rakesh. Yes, I know the truth. *You* know the truth. And now you know that I know the truth (as well as the position in which you configured those G.I. Joe figurines yesterday — boy, you dirty!). And guess what: It's fine. It's totally and completely fine, even if every time today that you imagine kissing a man you see yourself disintegrating into dust like that old Nazi at the end of *Indiana Jones and the Last Crusade*. Even if every time today you listen to "Vision of Love" you worry that there'll be a special place in Hell reserved for kids who buy Mariah cassette singles with loose change.

Even if every time today that you think the word "gay," you pray for it not to exist.

See, all those little things that you like to do, like drawing, painting, singing, organizing your Barbies according to level of décolletage — those are all helpful. The good adults in the world these days find those things amusing, especially in New York City, *where you live now.*

No, no, no, New York City doesn't look like those terrifying scenes in *Coming to America* anymore. It's nice now! Instead of run-down motels, there are hotels full of hot Europeans and fifteen-dollar donuts! Instead of metal bins coughing out smoke and fire, there are cupcake carts! Instead of *Cats*, there's no *Cats*! And most of all, instead of glares and muttered slurs everywhere, there are lots and lots and *lots* of gay people.

And you're one of them. When you go out on the weekends,

you're surrounded by friends, and many of them are gay too. There is a whole community out there that you haven't even seen yet, and I can tell you that a large number of those men know what it's like to try to re-create, in their own clothing, the cover of Paula Abdul's *Forever Your Girl*. (Oh, and about Paula . . . You know how Dad likes to point out that she's part Indian? Heads up: She'll be more talked about in fifteen years than the Taj Mahal.) Not everything is going to be perfect, and for every potential gay date that reminds you of a cute Kermit, there'll be one that gives you Miss Piggy nightmares. But I assure you that you are not alone. You are not going to crumble up and perish. You are not a weak kid. You are not . . . going to believe what people say to you when you wear those pedal pushers to class tomorrow.

But don't worry. You are not going to be scared forever either.

Love,

*Yourself*

P.S. No, really — love yourself.

P.P.S. Your best friend since fourth grade is gay. Just so you know.

# Doug Wright

*Dear Doug,*

I'm writing to you at a crazy time.

It's mid-October of 1980, and tonight — *in just a few short hours* — you're opening in the Highland Park High School senior play. You have the lead. (With a rakish streak of gray shoe polish in your hair, you'll essay the role of Henry Higgins in George Bernard Shaw's *Pygmalion* with a slight Texas accent and plenty of verve.)

On top of that, you have a quiz in AP History tomorrow. To burnish your resume for college applications, you're editing the literary magazine and even recording a book for the blind. And that's not all; your father wants you to mow the lawn.

Still, I hope you'll take time to read this note; I'm your older self, and I'm worried about you. You're trapped in a dizzying cycle of overachievement. It all looks good on paper, sure: the well-rounded go-getter, destined for immortality in the pages of the yearbook! But I know these compulsive strivings for what they really are: the manic efforts of a frightened boy seeking constant affirmation from the outside world in order to avoid confronting his true self.

You're running from secrets that have haunted you for years, some since grade school.

Your first crush wasn't Rosie Munroe, with her bubble-gum flavored lip gloss, or Amy Porter, who saucily snapped the straps on her training bra. No. It was Michael Edwards. Remember the pool party, where he wore pale blue trunks? He was golden and lithe, and the sight of the water coursing down his skin made you ache with longing.

Or what about the day in art class, when your favorite teacher referred to you as a "sissy boy" in front of all your peers? After school at the bike racks, a gang of jocks who happened to share her opinion beat you up and stole your backpack.

How about the pocket-sized Bible and flashlight you kept hidden under your mattress? When you had an erotic dream, you'd ward off images of Olympic swimmer Mark Spitz or movie heart-throb Ryan O'Neal by crawling under the bedspread and reciting psalms till morning.

What about that desperate day when — searching for knowledge that might offer you some comfort — you went rifling through your parents' bookshelf and discovered a self-help tome entitled *Everything You Always Wanted to Know about Sex but Were Afraid to Ask*? In the chapter on homosexuality, you learned that if you were (God forbid) actually gay, you would be condemned to a life of furtive bathroom encounters with strangers, and have a high propensity for suicide.

Have you forgotten that fateful morning in the shower when — with the water pressure full blast — you broke into tears and swore an oath to yourself: to carry these unsettling desires with you into the grave, even if it meant living a life absent romantic love altogether?

These incapacitating secrets govern you; they've forced you to live a life of denial, inhibition, and hyper-compensation. I've often wished that I could reach back in time, give you a consoling hug, and whisper, "It's going to be all right. Just *relax*."

So before you go onstage tonight, a few words of wisdom from your fiercest advocate.

> Stop working so hard to prove that you're worthy. Let appearances be damned. Make extravagant, reckless mistakes.

> You know Bruce Myers, the one kid in the neighborhood with the courage to come out of the closet at seventeen? Don't ostracize him; talk to him instead. *Whisper to him that you might be gay too.* You don't have to carry the truth close to your breast, like a secret stash of pills or a grenade; let it be a bridge to your own salvation and possibly his too.

Don't spend so much time in the mirror, cursing your DNA. I'll let you in on a secret: While you may not have a dimpled chin or six-pack abs, you are beautiful, because youth itself is beautiful, and time is too precious to waste on self-mortification.

Don't merely accept the fact that you were born gay; *treasure it*. You have a proud legacy: Alexander the Great, Michelangelo, Tchaikovsky, Gertrude Stein, Walt Whitman, Alan Turing, James Baldwin, Willa Cather, and Tennessee Williams, just to name a few.

Yes, the indignities you suffer at the hands of bigots can make you bitter. But they can also strengthen your ability to empathize with the oppressed, and in doing so, enlarge the capacity of your heart.

Live comfortably — *gratefully* — in your own skin.

I know that I'm asking you to incur substantial risk, so to tantalize you — and to offer encouragement when the path is dark and strewn with nettles — here are a few snapshots of your future. Let them be our secret. Pin them in your Drama Club binder, and only peek on the days you're hard-pressed to soldier on.

You're hosting a political fund-raiser in your Manhattan apartment; every candidate in the room is openly gay.

In a Los Angeles rental car, you're driving to pick up your wedding cake, and your mother says wistfully, "I always wanted all three of my children to be happily married; I just never imagined it would be the *gay one.*"

A breeze ripples your cabana on a beach in Mexico, as you celebrate your husband David's birthday. After eight years, his jokes are still the funniest and his approval means more than any sanction the anonymous world could ever provide.

You're protesting in Times Square for marriage equality. *Your own civil rights era has finally begun.* Despite your cynical nature, you know it's proof that — despite our prejudices, our capacity for cruelty in the guise of moral rectitude, and our chronic small-mindedness — mankind still lurches toward enlightenment.

That's all I'm going to say. I can't tell you more, because life should, life *must* carry some measure of surprise; I won't reduce yours to a laundry list. But if I'm content now — truly happy — it's because of you. It's because you've achieved a small miracle, far greater than getting the lead in a school play, or bringing home a Debate Team trophy, or chairing the Current Events Club. It's because you've managed to grow up gay in a hostile environment. That, my friend, is *huge*. So hang in there for both of us.

I won't keep you. Eliza Doolittle is waiting for her elocution lessons; you've a performance to give tonight, a role to play, one you've cultivated to a high sheen, a character you can safely inhabit without risk of exposure.

Between us, *let it be your last*.

Love (hard fought and hard won),

*D.*

# MELANIE BRAVERMAN

Thank you for being smart enough to forget that you drove
sixty miles to a bluegrass festival in Salem, Iowa
    that Sunday in June
when you were sixteen, Gospel Day, the Christians
    twangy and grateful
on the plywood stage before you on the crayon green grass
with your friend Jane Fett, track star, square-shouldered, beautiful
thank you for forgetting how you noticed
    the freckled sheen of Jane Fett's
skin that day, her blond curls, how the satin neck of her pink tank
dipped to a soft vee between her breasts, which were also pink
I know because you stumbled into a look at them then shot
to her chocolate eyes and back again a million thanks for forgetting
how you were overcome in that moment with the desire to kiss her
and for being so sure you were going to do it that you had to get up
and try to get yourself under control even though you didn't really
want to be controlled, allowing the three- and four-part harmonies
of the faithful to soothe you enough to buy a lemonade and go back

and be overcome again and like that until you got in the car
and drove home as if nothing ever happened
not the killing kind of forgetting but the waiting kind,
thank you for being so smart to forget about wanting
to kiss Jane Fett until you were two thousand miles
from your relentless home and finally free
for the first time in your life so lonely you made yourself
stand beside the hot pink azalea in your rented yard
and say hello to your next-door neighbor
who invited you in to meet her girlfriend
upon which a screen swung wide in your chest
that let the memory of wanting to kiss Jane Fett back in
because it had been waiting for you until the coast was clear
and you could from then on and always
remember who we really are.

# BRIAN SELZNICK

*(The first letter was written by Brian Selznick to his future self in 1980 when he was thirteen. The second letter was written to his younger self in 2011.)*

*March 27, 1980*
*Dear Brian,*

 *Hi! how are you? what was it like growing up and getting older? did you marry someone? is she nice? I'm in english with mr. pellechia. For math I have Allen (Boring) for social studies I have Rollis (jerk). For Reading I have Stocky (!). How old are you now? I'm 13. Today is Thursday and easter vacation is next week. I can't wait. Do you still wear glasses and have asthma? Colleen (remember her?) is sitting behind me. Remember Ginger and David, and andy and howie and carren lubowsky and Julie and how is Lee and Holly? How is Toto?, and Grandpa? Where are you living now? Remember Mike*

*Ploplis and Mal Blackwell and Mrs. Clevenger, what do you do for a living? Remember Todd gillman and amanda and Jess? Do you still like Mussells and drawing? Do you remember Charna and Jenn Beyes and Mrs. Sutton and Mr. Selick, David O Selznick, Bruce and Shelia, Jamie and Lisa Reiter remember Mr. Seel (6th) Mrs Sharkey (1st) mrs. Sherman (2nd) Mrs Dzelac (3rd) Mrs. Shisler (4th) Mrs. Dzelak and Mrs Sharpe and 6th Mrs Shisler*

*See ya around 1990,*

*Yours Truly,*

*You.*

February 12, 2011
Dear You,

I rediscovered your letter in my closet (an appropriate place to have found it, I guess) in 1988, the year I graduated college (I was twenty-one), so in fact I read the letter a few years earlier than I was supposed to. Even then I was shocked to have found it because I'd forgotten about it up until that point. I read the letter and put it back into my closet. I had all but forgotten about it again until I was asked to write a letter to my younger self for this book. I went back to my mom's house, but the letter was no longer in my old closet. Eventually I found it in a box of my things in the basement. The letter, like myself, had been liberated from the closet, it seems.

I'd like to answer the letter now, question by question, starting with the last one first.

1. Yes, I remember all my elementary school teachers. I could still name them all even without looking at the list you wrote.

2. I don't remember Lisa Reiter. Sorry, Lisa, whoever you are! I don't remember Jamie either, but Bruce and Sheila are my cousins, so yes, I remember them!

3. David O. Selznick was my grandfather's first cousin. He was a very famous producer of movies like the original *King Kong* and *Gone with the Wind*, so yes, I remember him.

4. Mrs. Sutton was my art teacher after school from the time I was in third grade until I graduated from high school. She was very important to me and my artistic education, and I will never forget her. A few years ago we reunited at the Museum of Modern Art in New York City where she'd taken me as a kid to see a Picasso exhibition. It was a thrill to walk around the museum with her again, talking about art. But Mr. Selick . . . who were you??

5. I do remember Charna, but not Jenn Bayes. I don't like mussels so much anymore, but I do still love to draw.

6. Todd Gilman was my next-door neighbor, and I

remember him and his sister Jennifer very well. He was my brother's friend, not mine really, so I'm not sure why I wanted to make sure I remembered him, but I do. Amanda and Jess, alas, have faded from my memory.

7. What do I do for a living? I write and illustrate children's books. I love what I do. I get to draw and research and travel, and it's a wonderful job. I'm very lucky.

8. I don't remember Mike Ploplis very well, but Mal Blackwell was a ginker. I thought everyone knew what a ginker was but when I got to college I found out that it's a term that seemed to be used only in East Brunswick, New Jersey. A ginker is someone who has long hair, wears a leather jacket, listens to heavy metal, and supposedly smokes a lot of pot. Mrs. Clevenger was an art teacher in middle school, and I remember hating her because she drew on my art without asking my permission. A few years ago I illustrated a book called *Frindle*, written by Andrew Clements, and I made the mean teacher look exactly like Mrs. Clevenger.

9. I live in New York and San Diego.

10. How are Toto and Grandpa? Not so well. Toto, our first pet, died in 1981 and Grandpa died in 1987.

11. Holly and Lee are my sister and brother, so, uh, yeah, I remember them pretty well. Holly and her husband,

Ed, have three boys and live in New Jersey. Lee and his wife, Sue, have three boys and a girl, and live in Virginia.

12.    I do remember Ginger. Her last name was Yoshimoro. David must refer to David Klein, who was my best friend when I was a kid. We are still friends. He lives in Texas with his family. Andy is Andy Levine, and yes, I remember him well. Howie is Howard Himmel, who lived up the block from me in East Brunswick. I heard he got married a few years ago and moved out of his parents' house. Carren Lubowsky was another neighbor. We used to love to make each other laugh. One time we made milk come out of our noses. I got in contact with her a few years ago. She's a lawyer now.

13.    I'm afraid I don't really remember Colleen, but I still wear glasses. My asthma is almost all gone, but I still have a little trouble breathing when I'm around animals, so I always carry some medication.

14.    Today is Saturday and Valentine's Day is next week.

15.    I'm forty-three.

16.    Did I marry someone? Is she nice? Well . . . this is the question that most surprised me, because I'm the only person who knows what you were really thinking at thirteen when you wrote it. You were already aware that there was something . . . wrong . . . with your interest in girls. I remember the girls you dated, like Lisa and Beth, but it never felt quite right. So it's

interesting to me that even though that was already in your head, you still assumed that you'd grow up and get married to a woman. Of course, you did phrase it as a question, so I guess you weren't *totally* sure you'd get married, but it's interesting nonetheless. So, to answer your question: No, I didn't get married to a woman, but I did fall in love. When I was thirty I started dating an incredible guy named David Serlin and we've been together for almost fourteen years now. Oh my gosh, I just realized that my relationship with David is a year older than YOU were when you wrote me your letter!

17. Is he nice? He's very nice. And patient and handsome and funny and brilliant.

18. What was it like growing up and getting older? Well, some of it was very hard, and some of it was great. When I first found your letter after college, I had only ever kissed one boy, and I was still pretty much in the closet. No one really knew I liked boys except a few close female friends from school. I felt a lot of shame about it for a long time. Why did that change? Well, I had great friends who were really supportive, and our family was supportive after a very difficult time trying to get Dad to understand (he did, eventually, although it took some doing!). I started dating, although before David my longest relationship was three months. Looking back now, I can say that

I've liked getting older. I feel more confident than I ever have before, and I've realized there's nothing to be ashamed of about being gay. I *like* being gay. I wouldn't change it for anything in the world.

19. How am I? I'm fine. Thank you for asking. And you will be too.

Love,

*Brian*

# STACEY D'ERASMO

*Dear Stacey,*

I see you so clearly, poetry-writing stoner girl that you are, the summer before college, in love simultaneously with an older man and the smartest girl in school (she really was), thinking that you have to choose, worried that you're too weird for him, not smart enough for her, talking it all over endlessly, filled with desire and ambitions you have no idea how to fulfill. You're kind of on fire and lonely at the same time, all the time. You listen to a lot of Joni Mitchell records. Also, you are worried that you are fat, and that you're a terrible driver, which is a serious liability in the suburbs. And you're beginning to be plagued by the anxiety that will shape-shift and goad you for many years to come. Here is what I want you to know that you don't know then: You're just as you should be. All that desire is going to turn out to be your compass in life, you are going to fall in love with incredible women, with incredible men, and they are going to fall in love with you.

You're going to have a wonderful time. You are going to discover again and again that your desire is an excellent guide; it knows when you're telling the truth and when you're not, and what you should do next, not only romantically, but also in figuring out what you want to do in this world. Your inability to lie about what you want — indeed, what some might call your excessive need to talk about it — and your strong wish to be recognized as you are will bring you extraordinary gifts and love and happiness and, through this honesty, you will find your way to the company of bold and generous people all your life. They will help you more than you can imagine. Okay, you're going to get in a little hot water now and then. Big deal. Honey: You can handle it. Even the anxiety, your devil, will have some useful aspects; like a Geiger counter, it will tick faster when you're in danger, even if the danger is on a psychically subatomic level.

Now, I have to tell you something else, which you are maybe not going to understand for a very long time. All tribes have their price. This isn't a failing, it's just the way tribes are. Please — and I know you're going to ignore me on this one — try to be more understanding toward yourself, more understanding of whatever tribe you're hanging with at any given time. No, the stoners don't understand the lesbians, and the lesbians and the gay guys don't always get along, and no one quite gets the bisexuals, and the literary world can be an unfair and prudish place. That is true. That's why I'm talking to the seventeen-year-old you, as you drive the wrong way up an exit ramp in your Dodge Dart Swinger, wondering who you should really love and who you're really going to be. The answer is: all of it. I could save you a lot of time if you would listen to me that this is it, you're already there, this is you. But you're not listening, because your boyfriend is yelling about the exit ramp situation and you're thinking about the red hair of the smartest girl in school. You need to keep your eyes on the road ahead.

I understand. I'll be here when you get here. I'll be so glad to see you. And, sweetheart, though you're not at all fat, you are, in fact, a terrible driver. Please move to New York soon for the safety of all concerned.

Much love,

*Stacey*

# ADAM HASLETT

*16 March 2011*

*Dear Adam,*

Greetings from the new age of insecurity. Living, as you are, back in the 1980s, you're no doubt still wondering if the world as you know it will end in nuclear war with the Soviet Union. But I'm writing to say that you will be spared that particular disaster. Our great fifty-year enmity, that prodigious engine of paranoia and fear, and the excuse for the bombing of villages and the backing of death squads, will evaporate before your eyes, and we will declare "victory" over our vanquished foe — a cynical old man of a system, it will turn out, who was dying from gangrene all along. But the reprieve from this compulsory dread, and the profitable misery that accompanies it, will, I'm afraid, be short. I know ten years seems like an eternity to you, a stretch of time you know only from reading novels, where a decade is a unit of aching regret in a stifled marriage or the span of an adult life before death in battle.

But decades do pass, moment by moment, day by day (you'll learn that), and by the opening of the twenty-first century, the city you'll come to live in will be shocked into rage and deep sadness by a spectacle of violence that will stun you. Its perpetrators will be postmodern religious fundamentalists. Not the sort you're living with now — the televangelists railing against abortion and the gay agenda, reinforcing the background militarism of American life, making the country safe for bullies and political thugs — but their rather more extreme Islamic counterparts, who also loathe modernity, and the sexual equality of women, and who see homosexuality as an abomination. Alas, then, I have to report that the political atmosphere of fear and manipulation, of war profiteers and false patriotism, will return with a vengeance as you pass into your thirties.

Right now, you're irate at the excesses of Reagan and Wall Street in your haughty, withering way. I'm afraid they will appear almost quaint in the course of time. You're growing up during an era when the rich are brasher than they've been in decades, conspicuous consumption is all the rage, and while you feel repulsed by it (not to mention above it), still, I know it seeps in. Money and success are the only things that seem to promise safety, especially given how entirely you feel locked out of the comforts of love. I'm sorry to say the rich will only get brasher, and the financiers will only get better at stealing the public's money, and the insecurities of young people reaching working age will only worsen.

Right now you're making $7.25 an hour scooping ice cream in Wellesley, Massachusetts. In twenty years, most everything will cost twice as much but that wage will remain the same (so be glad for what you're earning, my friend). As free market fundamentalism rages on, a whole lot of people will come out of the closet, you'll have sex in college, and plenty more afterward, and though it'll take a while, you'll have a boyfriend too. He'll be a med student and you'll be amazed he likes you and he'll teach you that sex doesn't always have to be so fraught and serious, that it can be a lark. And that will be an enormous relief, a gift he doesn't even know he's giving you, and luckily you'll be ready to receive it and hold on to it. From there, even after he's gone, things will be better because you'll realize you don't just have a mind, you have a body too, and it, or rather you, are capable of giving pleasure as well as receiving it. I know this matters more to you at the moment than politics because it seems much more closely tied to the chance of some barely glimpsed, ill-defined salvation from the intimate prison of loneliness and grief that you find yourself in. This prison will never vanish entirely. But it will become a ruin, with no walls left to hold you, a ghost of a place, always there in memory, and sometimes, strangely, almost comforting in its familiarity (beware its cold siren call on low days).

What you'll learn over the years is that while the love and sex and intimacy that seem so unattainable now can be glorious and sublime, they aren't the full answer to the riddle of your life. There's so much going on in your young mind, it seems almost unbearable, and you feel certain that if a cute boy would only hold you and kiss you, your fervid brain would go blissfully calm and all the world's problems would recede. But when you get older, and your heart has opened wide enough to let yourself be loved, you'll realize the opening doesn't stop there, at the door of the apartment you share with your boyfriend; it keeps going, opening to your friends and your aging family, into wars and politics, and sadness for your country, and, yes, sometimes despair. You see, love doesn't end despair. It deepens the poignancy of it by opening your eyes to what there is to lose. No matter how I describe this to you now, you can't understand it. Only time can do that to you.

If anything, I do wish I could tell you to enjoy yourself. Your worry doesn't help those you worry about, least of all yourself. It's a toothless clock wheel. You can let it stop and you'll be fine without it. You won't do this, I realize. After all, who's to say I've put it entirely aside myself? I just wish you knew that it *can* be put aside. Worries will only multiply, but your attachment to them can loosen. And that can make all the difference.

Finally, as cynical as your 1980s may be — "a low, dishonest decade," as Auden called the '30s — enjoy the pace of life you have now. You still write letters by hand. You call friends at home and if their phones are busy you call back later. You don't have a computer, much less the Internet. It's hard to appreciate absences, I realize. But perhaps this letter, typed on a laptop with email and twenty-four-hour-a-day news shot wirelessly from the heavens onto its screen, can help. Speed is all very sexy, and in our new age of insecurity it can often feel like the only way to stay ahead of the latest disaster at home or overseas. But information in excess becomes a fog and no matter how fast it rushes at you, it still obscures the actual landscape. So when you can, here and there, enjoy the dear old world as it was.

Best wishes,

*Adam*

# TERRENCE MCNALLY

*Dear Terry,*

I know you. Sex is the only thing we think about. While everyone else in Mrs. Lane's second-period Solid Geometry is puzzling out trapezoids, we're checking out the hair under Tommy Brown's arms and wondering when we're going to sprout some of our own. Sometimes he catches us looking at him and he rolls up the arms of his T-shirt one more turn. That's when we know it's time to lower our eyes and try to look at that trapezoid in front of us as if we meant it.

And every time Pete Welsh leans back at his desk and stretches, his T-shirt always rides up just enough in front to see that line of golden hair running from his navel down his belly to where it disappears under his 501s. We don't have a name for it but it's driving us crazy. It's called a Treasure Trail. We'll get one of our own any day now. It just won't be as beautiful or dangerous as Pete Welsh's.

Our school should be called Horny High.

At home, our nana has strong hands and can open jars of Smucker's that no one else in the family can and she always smells good when she hugs us, but we can't talk to her about sex. Our parents would freak out and our little brother's too young.

And sex is the only thing we want to talk about. No wonder: We're the only boy in the world who falls in love with other boys. We don't feel lonely; we have lots of friends. We feel alone, cut off, isolated, weird, maybe a little scared. Are we always going to be the only boy in the world who falls in love with other boys?

Having sex is never the problem. Nice girls don't put out at Horny High. It's easy to jack off with their disappointed boyfriends. Almost all of them are up for that. No big deal. It's what straight guys do. Except we aren't straight guys. We're the editor of the school paper and having sex with our friends is what we do. It's a perfect arrangement.

It's what comes after that we're beginning to hate: the pretending that it hadn't happened. You know, we were both drunk or we were just fooling around. Whatever you call it, we weren't making love.

When you're in love you kiss and you look the other person in the eye and tell them you love them and you would do anything in the world for them, even die.

But this, what we do with other boys, can never be acknowledged or talked about, ever. He will go to his grave first. Don't look at him, pull your pants up, and get in the car.

We don't feel ashamed when we get home. We feel empty. We drink a Coke. We smoke a Lucky Strike. We fall asleep thinking about James Dean and how we would kiss him on the lips and tell him we loved him. With Jimmy it would be so much more than tonight. He would kiss us back and he would tell us he loved us too — but only if he did. Jimmy isn't a liar.

When I was your age — and that was a lifetime ago — the last people I wanted to hear from were old ones, which is what I am now.

You will grow up. Adolescence will be a distant, but always a vivid, memory. You will meet the one other boy in the world who falls in love with other boys. Maybe you won't fall in love but you will kiss each other on the lips and you won't pull your pants up the moment you're done.

You will meet more and more only boys in the world who love other boys. Then, if you're lucky, and you're out, really out, 24/7, and you're comfortable with who you are, you will meet Tom Kirdahy and you will kiss each other on the mouth and tell each other "I love you" and you will mean it and you will be able to marry and have a family and you can both go about the wonderful business of the rest of your life.

I love you. I envy you. We will always have Horny High.

xxxx

*Terrence McNally*

# ERIK ORRANTIA

*Dear Faggot,*

Well, that's what you are, isn't it? Why else did you have the hots for your first girlfriend's ex-boyfriend? You were supposed to get jealous, but you couldn't resist his slender legs in those tapered jeans, his masculine jaw, his rebellious nature, or the package at his crotch. They say everyone has a bad boy phase. Didn't realize it would apply to you. But you kept the urges inside, hidden from the rest, the ones who would have told you what a faggot you were.

Remember those kids at outdoor education camp? I know, some of them were cute, but that's not what I'm talking about. They put you up on that stump and told you, in an act of faith, a team-building exercise, to fall back into their waiting, crisscrossed arms. You were the only one who wouldn't do it. You did not have faith in them. You were not part of the team.

You didn't really know, though, or were afraid to admit that something strange was bubbling inside you, beneath your perfect, shiny shell. Fear kept it inside and tried to squelch that bubbling for so long, along with all your other emotions. But, like when you were six and got caught peeing between the dressers for no apparent reason, what flowed inside had to come out. It took you a while.

The first image you saw of gays shown on the television was that of Sister Boom Boom, a drag nun of the Sisters of Perpetual Indulgence, leading the gay pride parade in her humongous habit and her magnificent makeup. Not unlike current times, the reporter forgot to mention that the Sisters, a charity organization, used drag to call attention to various forms of sexual intolerance — homophobia, discrimination against those with HIV/AIDS, and other gender issues. They surely also forgot to pan across to the other folks in the parade, all as normal or abnormal as the rest of society. As you watched the news that day, you felt as if you had just walked into an adult-only movie. Mom promptly and indignantly shut the TV off, protecting the eyes and ears of her young faggot-to-be.

Several years later you found yourself listening to the songs of Erasure with the speakers turned down to about one decibel. Incredible! Even at that low volume, the lyrics of "Hideaway" blared out, as if they were singing about you, or singing to you: *One day the boy decided, to let them know the way he felt inside . . .* When Mom did find out, though, she probably would have preferred for you to pee between the dressers again. First she cried. Then, she "loved the sinner but hated the sin." And later, she taught you that people can change at any age. "Who am I to judge?" she said to you not that long ago, and, "Did I ever tell you I was sorry?" Sometimes things get worse before they get better, but they do get better.

Finally, "faggot" became a label that you were proud of. Now, you wouldn't have it any other way. In reality, what frightens you most is often what you ought to do. If you've learned anything, it's that the ignorance persists. It doesn't mean you speak out or fight every time you hear it. One has to pick her battles. But it does mean you never let their fear take anything away from you, or make you less than what you are.

So now being a faggot isn't such a terrible thing. It reminds you that we are everywhere, that we will prevail, and that we have a lot to be proud of. There is so much more about you to be proud of besides being gay, but somehow sexuality posed the Mount Everest of life's obstacles — once you conquered it, you could conquer anything else.

Okay, so now you are over forty. Always thought you would have had everything figured out by now, right? Didn't happen. But you have survived enough hard times to appreciate the good ones. You try to keep it simple and not worry about trifles. You try to let go of the things you can't control. You try to give your part, or more. You try to show people the same acceptance you wish they would show you. You try to have faith. Though you don't always succeed in these things, or may not always know how, you never stop trying. You try to fall back on the team once in a while. How else would you have become an accomplished teacher, counselor, writer, Ping-Pong player, life partner, Spanish speaker, and faggot?

Affectionately,

*Erik Orrantia*

68

69

# MARTIN MORAN

*Dear One,*

You were only twelve when it started. I know. You'd never had sex of any kind. You didn't have a hair on your body except what was on your head. You knew something mighty was on its way. You were waiting for the big dream, the trigger. The one they mention in Sex Ed or Biology. Wet dream. First splash of sperm — magic-gonna-be-a-MAN! potion. You'd heard about it, read about it, in the back of the scout book. Nature taking its course. But it was all thrown off course. You allowed the dream to be stolen.

Or so you feel. So you believe. And so it hurts and haunts like mad. I know.

It began (Remember? 'Cause I know you're crazy busy burying it, hiding it, forgetting it. I know you are sure you could never *ever* speak of it) when a friend from the neighborhood, a fellow paper-boy, Catholic kid like you, asked if you wanted to go on a weekend trip. He knew a cool dude, a counselor from the church camp, who was fixing up a ranch, a special summer place for boys.

"A ranch? Wow!"

The counselor needed help. "Pays ten bucks," your friend said.

"Cool!"

You got permission from Mom and off you went on a Friday afternoon. It was April, wildflowers blooming. You drove high into the Rockies past patches of snow in a yellow International Harvester. And that first night while your buddy slept, the cool, tall dude, who knew the names of constellations, who could spot a spruce from a cedar, a Hereford from a Holstein, he pulled you into his sleeping bag. It was late and dark and he was so warm and oh God you let him. He slipped off your underwear and touched you and you came for the very first time. The pleasure of it so deep and sharp it cut right to heaven and back and you knew right then you were damned. Ruined.

It went on for three years, the sex. Top secret. A wild need inside growing larger as your small body grew tufts of hair, your bones got bigger and your voice deepened. He was the one soul who knew, who knew what you really were: swollen bad with desire. He was the only relief from the guilt of having let it all happen.

You couldn't hold it anymore, the secret that hummed and hounded — hounds you still, I know. First, you tried with pills you'd stolen from Mom's medicine chest. You barfed all over the bedroom carpet. That didn't do the trick so one night — you were fifteen — you found the twenty-two rifle that Dad had left behind when he moved out. You found the bullets in the middle drawer of the bureau in the basement. Brought them to your room, to your desk where all your homework sat screaming to be done. You loaded the gun, put the barrel to your temple, reached for the trigger. You were naked and shaking with anger. You decided better throw on pajamas so they won't find you this way: on the orange carpet, in a pool of blood, new patches of hair hanging out. So you dressed and sat back down and put the barrel to your head. What else, you think, could blot out the blackness of the sin hidden beneath your altar boy robes. Your finger was there but the moment you squeezed the trigger (still not sure how it happened) a hand, an instinct, *your angel-gut*, that deepest part of you that knows *you want life,* you want to see what will come, that part *yanked* the rifle. The bullet blasted through the paneling of the bedroom wall and through the banister of the basement steps and ended up somewhere in the storeroom.

Young one, your secret is here. It is safe. It is ours and we are living. The thoughts of suicide still dog you, I know, but you'll do me this favor, won't you? Throw away the bullets; flush away the pills. One day (sooner than you think!) you will know that what you're hiding isn't you, one day what seems so heavy will weigh so little you feel you might fly. Because the very thing you are hiding, the very pain that throbs in your breast turns out to be your finest, fiercest teacher.

One day, can you believe? You will write a book about what happened. An award-winning book about the secret sex, how it brought you richest pain and knowledge even as it nearly killed you. How you learned that forgiveness was a gift you would give to yourself. The book will even be funny because your life turns out to be full of funny and full of good. You *know* this, don't you? Deep inside. It turns out good. Complicated and sad and difficult, yes. But good.

Listen, young one. You're fine. From your gut to your groin you know what you're doing. Except when you don't. And that's fine too. One day you'll know that every step happened just the way it did so that you would land exactly where you were meant to be.

You'll go to college, you'll sing. One day you'll meet a man whose eyes are so startling you understand you'll never know the end of him. So you take him into your arms and walk through life together. And on your twenty-fifth anniversary the two of you visit Paris (a city you've walked together many times) and you stay in a room overlooking the Seine and on your last night in town, a snowy eve — Feast of the Epiphany — you happen upon a little cinema. By chance, your favorite movie is playing there and you go in and watch and when you hear the film's final words —

*His soul swooned slowly as he heard the snow falling faintly through the universe*
*and faintly falling, like the descent of their last end upon all the living and the dead.*

— you both cry so hard that you laugh so loud as you walk out to get a midnight coffee hearing all the while the lilt of Joyce's lines in your head grateful, grateful that you are among the living.

I know that right now you feel it's impossible that you could speak, that *anyone* could hear, that anyone could understand the story hidden in your gut but soon, any moment, you will find a way to lift your head and turn to the faces around you — the redheaded singing teacher; the mother of your classmate Theresa. You'll speak of what's inside. You can take care of yourself this way. You'll see you do not need to carry it alone. You can write it down. You can ask for help. You can even call across the wire- less where men and women just like you are on the other end. They will not judge. They can hold just as much of your secret as you wish to share. They know about secrets, they've had their own and they know *it's not your fault;* that you're just a kid doing a kid's job — falling into love, falling into life.

And, dear boy, do this, please. When you finish reading this letter, walk over and look into the mirror and take a breath — I am serious — breathe and look there to see the fierce young man who will travel miles and who will help so many because of the pain that taught him about being human. Look at your face, your eyes; your sweet, good body, and behold the greatest secret of all. Look there, at the boundless strength. You see? No kidding, friend.

With love,

*Marty*

# Armistead Maupin

*Dear Me,*

Remember when you knew there was no turning back?

It was a muggy summer afternoon in Raleigh, and you had just dropped off your grandmother at the beauty parlor in the old Carolina Hotel on Nash Square. Killing time, you had wandered into the newsstand — the "blind stand," as it was called back then, since it was run by a blind man — and you and this sightless cashier were the only people in the room. There's no way he could have known where your eyes were fixed so feverishly, but you wondered if he was already on to you. What if his handicap had heightened his other senses? What if the mere sound of your footsteps had betrayed your exact location and the object of your lust?

You could easily have flipped through that magazine. Hell, you could have *bought* the damned thing. You could have told him it was *Time* or *Field & Stream*, and he would have been none the wiser. But you were so scared that you just left it there unexplored, fleeing the newsstand with a feeble "thank you, sir" to make it clear to him that you hadn't been shoplifting. It wasn't until you had reached the safety of your car (your *first* car, that cherry red VW) that you could let yourself reassemble the image that had so undone you. You had seen photos of shirtless men before — in the Sears catalog, for instance — but the guy on the cover of *Demigods* magazine, he of the oaken arms and golden chest, had not been there in the name of haberdashery; he'd been lolling in bed amid a tangle of silver satin sheets.

You turned on the car radio to collect yourself, only to hear a song called "Walk on the Wild Side," which seemed the perfect theme music for the moment, since it proclaimed with sultry trombones that you had already begun your long slide into hell. How could you argue with that? Apparently there were whole magazines out there devoted to your secret mental illness, or, as the state of North Carolina liked to put it, your "abominable crime against nature."

Okay, stop. Here's what I want you to know, son:

Forty years after that queasy epiphany you'll tell a friend this story, and he'll smile knowingly. The next day he'll come to your house with an old issue of *Demigods* — not just any issue either, *the very one* — and you'll see that your heartthrob had been just as beautiful as you remembered (the arms, the chest, that rakish curl across his forehead), though his name (Larry Kunz) will leave a little something to be desired. As for those silver satin sheets, they'll prove not to be sheets at all but a plastic shower curtain wrapped around his waist. He's not even in bed, in fact — that's a bathtub he's sitting on. Never mind. He's all yours now, for as long as you want.

But you're wondering, of course, what you'll find *inside* the magazine. Alas, no more photos of Mr. Kunz, but lots of other young bucks with names like Troy Saxon and Mike Nificent, decked out in posing straps and sailor caps. You'll also appreciate the page of mail order gifts, exotic items apparently indispensable to the manly household of 1962: An Indian pith helmet, an antique dealers' handbook, a 21-inch imported Italian peppermill, a musical cigarette box that played "Smoke Gets in Your Eyes."

And what will strike you most about this fading artifact is how brazenly innocent it seems to you now. You'll be hard pressed to recall how it had once filled you with scorching shame, invoking that ominous war chant of a word — ho-mo-sex-u-al — you'd been trying so hard not to hear. But you could never have known then that what you feared most in yourself would one day become the source of your greatest joy, the very foundation for your success.

Which is why, when *Demigods* finds its way back to you, you will frame it and hang it on your kitchen wall. It will stay there for years, a souvenir of bygone fears and a source of daily amusement to you and the man you married.

Love,

*Armistead*

# ARTHUR LEVINE

*Dear Arthur,*

Maybe you could have used this letter when you were a *little* kid. Remember the rule your mom had that you couldn't play with a girl for two days in a row after school? You had to find a boy to rotate in? Your parents were too sophisticated to come right out and say, "Boys don't play with girls. Boys don't play with dolls. Boys are supposed to *chafe* at rainy days; they don't prefer to stay inside and draw. Boys like throwing balls, not playing hopscotch. Or talking." They just implied it. I guess they might have even thought that a *little* nonconformity was OK, but they were clearly worried that you were pushing the limits of what would be seen by others as acceptable. And I know you felt that worry, and that it became YOUR worry. I would have stepped right in there, put an arm around your shoulders, and reassured you. I would have said, "It is totally fine for almost all your friends to be girls. You will grow up and work in a field that is 98 percent female. The pleasure you get from talking to girls will make your work life (not to mention the rest of your life) a thousand times happier. The fact that you 'like girls' will be a problem for exactly thirteen seconds in the relative time frame of your life. Also: Go ahead and play the Scarlet Witch during superhero fantasy games if you think her powers are cooler and her costume more fun." Then I would have taken you to A&S Department Store or Gimbels and bought you a Barbie doll. And then driven us to Carvel's afterward.

Of course I didn't get to say those things to you when you were little, and no one else did. So you learned to hide those sissy impulses, as if they were a bright pink parka stuffed in the back of your closet behind the carefully chosen blue and brown clothing, only peeking out occasionally, and quickly stuffed back again.

It turns out to be the things you *couldn't* hide so easily that bring you the most trouble. In junior high there are some kids who find out you are a Jew and pitch pennies at you in the hall to see if you'll pick them up. Other kids will try to humiliate you by shouting, "BRAIN!" (a multi-syllable word in their nasal, Long Island accents) as if you should be embarrassed to have known the answers to the questions the teacher was asking in the last period. And of course you ARE embarrassed, despite "knowing better."

When the football players steal your street clothes during the high school variety show rehearsal and throw them in the garbage, where you find them hours later, it isn't because you're gay (your girlfriend is rehearsing with you when this happens), but because you're Jewish and smart AND maybe-a-hint-of-something-gay. . . .

It's their vague sense that you're different and vulnerable and threatening.

But the scars from this are tiny and faint. Much more important, these experiences give you a small sense of what it's like to be bullied. And it gives you a lifelong identification with the underdog. With books in particular, you are drawn to stories where a person has hidden talents, unappreciated skills, a great destiny perhaps. Remember the name Harry Potter.

In the meantime, I know that you never REALLY think it's a bad thing to be smart, or to be a Jew. You know in your heart that "they" were wrong. And this will help you with the gay thing eventually — just to know that other people could be very certain about how awful something about you was, and still be way off the mark.

But here are some things that I know you need assurance about right now:

Your parents: Oh, honey, coming out to your parents will be hard. In fact, it won't be you who initiates it, it'll be them. In your freshman year of college they will start dropping hints. You will have this exchange with your mother over the telephone (repeatedly):

Mom: You know, Arthur, if you ever feel the need to TALK to someone . . . if something is BOTHERING you, we will gladly pay for you to see a psychologist.

You: Thanks, Mom, I'm fine. Do YOU want to see a psychologist? You know YOU can see a psychologist if you're worried about something.

This will happen so often that you will retreat to the safety of the library in the Sarah Doyle Women's Center at your school, where they have a special shelf of books about coming out to your family. (Yes, the women's center — you still like playing with girls.) You will read every book twelve times as if you are preparing for a test that you desperately want to ace.

But then one night, at the beginning of summer vacation, you will come home and retreat to your room to write in your journal. There will be a knock on your door. And a request: "Arthur, we want you to come to the living room." (You will know this is bad: Yours is not the kind of family that has formal talks in the living room.)

And it is bad, though it also plays out almost exactly as the books said it would. Your parents run through clichés of what parents say to children who are coming out: "How can you know if you haven't slept with a girl?" (You will reply, "I don't know, Mom, how do *you* know you're straight if you haven't slept with a girl?")

"Why are you doing this to us?"

"What did we do to YOU that has made you this way?"

And worst of all, toward the end of the multi-hour conversation:

"You can change if you want to. We'll pay for a psychologist to help you."

Ah, the psychologist again.

Because you have studied, and because you are prepared, and because of all the self-confidence and strength, ironically, that your parents have given you, you will manage to tell them, "I can't change this part of me. And I don't want to. I will agree to see a psychologist, but only as part of family therapy — that is, only if you agree to see one too. This is not MY problem, it's YOUR problem, and we need help getting over it."

Those are strong words, but you are not in a position of strength. You are dependent on your parents, and so they choose the psychologist, a friend of the rabbi who heads your Jewish Center.

You endure two or three sessions with him where he tries to convince you that you can become heterosexual if you try very, very hard, and he probes your psyche for weaknesses, for a lever to turn you to his way of thinking.

Finally he says: "Why is it that you admit you are nervous about coming out to your friends and that you're afraid that they won't accept you . . . and yet you seem to think your parents *will* accept you?"

You say: "Because my friends don't HAVE to be my friends. My parents have no choice but to be my parents, and so I have to believe that they will accept me for who I am, eventually."

He says: "I think you are being totally unrealistic."

You say: "Then we have nothing further to talk about."

He says: "OK . . . well, let's put our next session on the calendar. What day shall we meet?"

And you say: "Never."

Arthur, you will in fact never have to see that idiot quack snake-charm salesman again. And the most important thing I can tell you is that although that guy certainly didn't help your parents (and probably set the process back a few years) he was totally and utterly wrong about them.

It will take a good long decade after that first terrible coming out conversation. (Hang on, Arthur, I swear.) There will be years where the tension between you and your folks will be nearly unbearable. But very, very gradually, it will begin to ease.

When you are twenty-eight you will start dating a guy who is not only handsome and smart and hysterically funny, but who is also a doctor (and can therefore talk to your father about the one thing your father can talk about).

A giant breakthrough will occur three years later (1993) when the two of you decide to get married. At the ceremony, on a beautiful lawn overlooking the Hudson River, your parents will watch you, surrounded by friends you've known all your life. (Did I mention that you were wrong to worry about your friends? You don't lose a single one when you come out. Not even the big straight soccer boy you are madly in love with. You only get closer.) They see these friends, and your work colleagues of all ages, and your extended family, and everyone is beaming, and everyone is happy, especially you. And it turns out that this is really all they truly wanted: to see you happy. They just didn't realize you could be gay AND happy.

The choke-knots of tension slip open, never to be retied. They are present at your first, and fifth, and tenth, and twentieth anniversaries. They are overjoyed at the birth of your son.

Things work out with your parents, Arthur. You find love. And you get to play with girls just as often as you want.

*Love, Arthur*

# MALINDA LO

*Dear Malinda, Age 16:*

Do you remember, when you were six years old, how Dad used to wake you up in the morning? He would play the record of Disney's *Cinderella*, your favorite movie. (It's OK to admit it. You were six.) The strains of "A Dream Is a Wish Your Heart Makes" would tremble down the hallway of the house on Doric Drive, and you would wake up imagining ballrooms and billowing gowns and Prince Charming.

I remember.

It's a lovely dream: to have a fairy-tale romance. But dreaming that dream has a consequence too. The consequence is yearning. It hurts, doesn't it? But it feels good too. The hollow center inside you, the wanting of someone to love you. The ache makes your heart race as if you really were in love.

But you're not. Not yet.

Sophomore year, when that boy Steve drove you to school every morning in his Bronco II, you were so willfully ignorant of what that might mean. It wasn't until you got those tickets to *Romeo and Juliet* at the Colorado Shakespeare Festival — *Romeo and Juliet!* — and asked him if he wanted to go, and when he picked you up he was drenched in cologne — *then* you knew.

I remember.

It was June: a warm and dry summer evening. Later, the sun would set over the Rocky Mountains in a typically extravagant display of orange and pink against a violet sky. A perfect night.

He got out of the car and rang the doorbell. He met your dad, who shook his hand. He smelled like a *date*. One of those boy-arrives-with-flowers, takes-you-to-a-romantic-play kind of dates. It was the weirdest, most awkward moment of your life. Sure, you'd had a crush on him in fifth grade, but this was five years later, and presented with the option of romance, you completely froze. Terrified, you talked all night about your friend Brian, who, I should note, will turn out to be gay. (I know you won't believe me.)

But Steve didn't know that. You could practically see him shrinking away bit by bit as you gushed about Brian, until the foot and a half between you two in his Bronco at the end of the night could have been a mile. It's not surprising that he ended up dating your friend Nicole instead of you. (Nicole is a whole other story that I won't get into right now, but suffice it to say, she's not exactly straight either. I know, you're like: What does *that* mean? Wait for it.)

I know that you feel like you completely messed up that night. You had this chance in the palm of your hand, and you not only threw it away, you threw it away in the face of the person who offered. It wasn't your finest moment. But I know why you did it. Because the possibility of love terrifies you. It's something that you yearn for while running from it.

I will tell you something that those fairy tales don't. You're right to be terrified. Love, in the fullness of its power, will turn you inside out. And maybe, right now, you're not ready for it yet.

I know that you desperately want someone to love you, to see you for who you are and to not only appreciate that but to buoy you up, floating. I promise you it will happen. A day will come when your fear will crumble in the face of a need to leap into the unknown that is love. Wait for it.

One last thing: Yes, your dreams will come true, but you're not going to marry a prince.

Love,

*Malinda, Age 36*

# MAURICE VELLEKOOP

Dear Maurice in Grade 9:

Is that a boy or a girl?

Labatts

With tenderest compassionate sympathy I write to you from your own future with incredible news!

THISTLETOWN COLLEGIATE INSTITUTE

Furiously trying to hold books by your side like a guy, not across your chest

Would you believe: There'll come a time when you don't ever have to even visit the suburbs?

cocksucker

faggot

That one day you'll be surrounded by an international cast of sexy, urbane, multi-talented friends?

That you'll have a decades-spanning career as a celebrated illustrator and author?

Working for my dad at the Christian school I attended from grades 1 to 8

That you could enjoy sexuality without the guilt and shame of the Christian Reformed Church?

The only private space in a family of 6

Maurice Vellekoop

# MICHAEL NAVA

*Dear Mike,*

Y ou are about to turn fourteen and begin one of the hardest years of your life. The reason is not that you will discover you are a homosexual — you've known that for a couple of years now, since you burrowed into the stacks of the main library in downtown Sacramento and found the books that described and gave a name to your feelings about other boys. Those books, which you continue to read secretly, never taking them far from the shelves, do not give you much hope about your "condition." Most of them are texts on abnormal psychology that describe homosexuals as sort of hysterical half-women who live in the shadows and prey on the unsuspecting, more like vampires than human beings. You do not recognize yourself in these descriptions and you do not want to believe that this is what you will become when you grow up. You want to be a lawyer and to help people, and you cannot understand how someone with that ambition could become one of the shadowy, sad creatures described in these texts.

Still, because books have been your door out of your family's difficult life, you trust the information they provide to you. All of this has left you confused. What will now happen, Mike, is that you will fall in love for the first time with a boy in your class. You have known him for a couple of years and consider him a casual friend. But when school begins in September, you will look at this boy and see him in a way you never have before. You will notice that his eyes are not just brown, but complicated with faults of yellow and black, and that the texture of his skin is unusually smooth. You will notice the slightly hoarse tone of his voice and a dozen other things about his physical presence that will make it seem to you, when you are with him, as if there is no one else in the world but the two of you. You will feel a yearning toward him that will keep you awake at night and a happiness when you are together that you have never felt with anyone.

In the course of the next year, you will also suffer greatly because this sweet, amiable boy will have no idea of the depth of your feelings for him and no ability to return them. There will be no one in whom you confide the reason for your unhappiness, and your pain will seem unbearable to you. Harder yet, you will wonder if it will always be this way — if you will be condemned to love people who can't love you back. You will think if that is to be the case, maybe it would be easier not to go on living because you cannot imagine there will ever be a place for you in this small central California city you call home.

There is nothing I can tell you that can change these events.

What I can tell you, though, is that there are lessons in this experience, as hard as it will be, that will ultimately give you the courage to make a better and happier life.

You will learn that the books that pretend to describe homosexuals are wrong because to be a homosexual is not to want to sexually prey on others, but to love another and to be loved. Your fantasies with that boy are not sexual fantasies but romantic ones — to hold hands as you walk with him between classes, to kiss him, to hold him. They are no different than the fantasies of the boys and girls around you who are beginning to pair off into couples. You believe now that in their world, in the world at large, there is no place for someone with your longings. But soon you will have to make a decision — to hide who you are and be who the world wants you to be, or to trust yourself and to be yourself even though you do not know how you will do that.

You will choose to trust yourself. You will not pretend to like girls — that would be dishonest and you like your friends too much to use them that way. You will keep quiet and wait. You will wait in hope that the day will come when there will be someone for you with whom you can experience the love you felt for your friend, and who will return it.

Mike, that day will come. Sooner than you think. And you, because you said no to what the world told you about being gay, will have helped bring that day to pass. You will take your pain and convert it into words — all the words you are unable to say now — and write the kind of books about being gay you wish you had found on the shelves of the Sacramento Central Library for others to find, to help lighten their loads. You will become a lawyer and work for your own equality and the equality of others like you. Best of all, you will find your friend, your companion, your partner. Keep going, Mike. I'll meet you on the other side of fourteen.

Love,

*Michael*

# LARRY DUPLECHAN

*Hey, Kiddo.*

Greetings from the twenty-first century. This is a message to you, from you. Well, you're *going* to be me: This is from you in your fifties.

I know; at seventeen years old, fifty sounds ancient. But believe me, fifty will be here before you know it. The good news is, you're going to age pretty darn well (when you get a moment, you should thank Mom for those cheekbones). And, you're gonna have pecs. Actual *pecs*. Hard to imagine when you're tipping the scales at one hundred twenty pounds and Bill Ware (who'd be kind of cute if he wasn't such a huge jerk) recently described you as "kinda scrawny"; but the time will come when coworkers will call you "Muscles." I swear. You're probably rolling your eyes, or laughing, or both. But that's okay. These abs don't lie.

Congratulations on surviving high school. I know it hasn't been easy for you, a small, effeminate, artsy Black boy stuck in a rednecky Mormon-y little town, in a high school without so much as an auditorium. But I have more good news: You'll be able to take your memories of those four years of misery and hell, and turn them into a critically acclaimed novel; so try to remember everything. And take heart: Real Life is *nothing* like high school. Starting with college, very few people will care that you can't throw a baseball. Soon, you'll meet people who actually value your intelligence and talents, people who'll understand your cultural references and get your jokes, people who have seen *Stage Door* and know who Bette Midler is. Remember the year-end choir concert, after your solo number ("And I Love You So," which you learned from Helen Reddy's *I Am Woman* album), when the audience applauded, and kept applauding, filling the multipurpose room with the sound of their approval, and you thought your heart might explode inside you? You'll have a lot more moments like that one.

Oh, you'll have bad moments. Baby, you're gonna have some bad *years*. After you come out to them, Mom will call you vicious, ugly things, and Dad will — well, let's just say he'll make your life difficult; and you'll think you'll never be able to forgive them. But you will forgive them — though that will take some time. And their attitudes will change — though, again, that will take some time. Years later, you'll experience grief the likes of which you can't even imagine now — you'll watch your best friends die young, from a disease with no cure. But you'll get through it, I promise. You're stronger than you know; stronger than you'd ever dream. And don't worry: You won't be alone through this.

Which brings me to Frank Pryor: enough listening to "I Honestly Love You" by Olivia Newton-John over and over, and crying. There's just no percentage in falling in love with straight boys. There's a Gay Students' Union at UCLA: You'll meet more than enough *gay* boys to develop crushes on. And in your sophomore year — no, I won't spoil it for you. I'll just say, not to worry: You'll have dates, and trysts, and affairs. And you *will* find love. You'll fall in love with someone, and he'll fall in love right back. Matter of fact — no, I shouldn't. Yeah, I will:

Before you're through, you're going to get married to a man. I mean really, legally married. To a *man*.

Oh yes: and the President of the United States is Black.

Fine, *don't* believe me. Just get through this summer as best you can. And remember: incline bench presses. Trust me.

Love,

*Larry*

# ALI LIEBEGOTT

*Dear Ali,*

Even if you did nothing but algebra homework for the next three months, there's still no mathematical way you could catch up. So stop worrying. None of this will even matter a year from now. It's fruitless to wish for earthquakes or fires to destroy the entire school just so you will be free from taking your algebra test tomorrow. You know who should waste their life doing algebra homework: happy, budding mathematicians — not people like you who, after they look at an equation, walk in a small circle like a decrepit, arthritic dog, and groan as they lie down to sleep.

You are not a happy, budding mathematician, Ali. You are a depressed, closeted queer stuck in a town with no resources or allies. Plus, your wardrobe consists of maternity-style jumpers your mother sewed for you even though you're not a pregnant teen.

Don't worry about your biology homework either. You're not

going to be a biologist even though you considered it for one second when you learned that cells could commit suicide. Apoptosis — cellular suicide. The cell offs itself before it divides because it knows it's mutated and doesn't want to pass on the mutation to its offspring. How considerate. You can appreciate the poetics of apoptosis and use it for online passwords or an impressive Scrabble move now and then but that doesn't mean you're a biologist either. Apoptosis works for cells but not people, okay, Ali? What do they say about suicide — it's a permanent solution to a temporary problem. Suicides can look like a lot of things. Sometimes suicide just looks like only drinking Diet Cokes for all your meals or driving a car, drunk, straight into a tree. BLAM! That's it. Someone's going to die like this before you graduate, but it doesn't have to be you.

Get a handful of good friends who don't care about your maternity jumpers. You know what good friends do? They say, "Meet me on the baseball field tomorrow at midnight." Instead of trying to catch up on any of your fifty-three missed algebra assignments, I encourage you to go to that visitor's dugout and join them in a great school prank. You'll climb over the chain-link fence and into the high school, and while the school is dark, armed with Krazy Glue and a backpack full of rolled pennies, together you will glue a penny over the keyhole of every classroom door, so the next day when the faculty arrives, under-caffeinated and stressed out, one by one, they'll put a key into the impenetrable side of a copper penny. Haha! Can you see those groggy teacher faces now, calling out one by one to each other, "Hey, is there something wrong with your lock too?" A locksmith will have to be called. It will take hours for all the pennies to be pried off. School's canceled! It's not your fault you live in California and don't get snow days. Sometimes a person has to make their own snow day! It's the miracle you'd prayed for to save you from your algebra test!!! And, Ali, just between us, it's the thing that teachers pray for too. A real win-win situation.

Promise me this, Ali — no apoptosis attempts and pay attention in your typing class. One day, you'll want to tell your story and it will help if you don't have to hunt and peck.

XOXOX,

*Ali*

P.S. Don't try and jump that fence in that maternity jumper. Put on some sweatpants.

# PAUL RUDNICK

*Dear young Paul,*

You've known you were gay since approximately three seconds after you were born, because when the obstetrician slapped you, you said, "Stop that." You've also always known that, after a perfectly respectable childhood, you would leave the New Jersey suburbs and move to New York City, not because you were gay, but because you were sane. Since all of that's been taken care of, I'd like to let you in on a few more developments:

1.  All of the people in your high school whom you hope will turn out to be gay, meaning assorted jocks and the hunkier teachers, will all remain straight. You already know who the gay folks are: They're the sadly ordinary, dweeby boys and girls just like you. But here's a bonus: As adults, some of the dweebs will start working out and will begin to resemble those

jockier fetish objects, without having to actually play team sports. Other gay guys, as adults, will begin to play and enjoy team sports, and they will become just a bit too proud of this. In addition, most of those heterosexual fetish objects will peak sometime around high school graduation, and their waistlines will expand as their hairlines contract, which is when you can hear God giggling.

2.   You will discover that all gay men are not stylish, witty, promiscuous, and viciously entertaining. No one said that equality was going to be fun.

3.   You will work in the theater, where you will meet many talented and delightful people. Be grateful, and always tell these people that they are geniuses, because this is how theater people say hello.

4.   People have been claiming, and writing, that they are post-gay since the beginning of time.

5.   Anyone who says that they don't like the word *gay*, or that they hate labels, or that they're not gay, they're a person: That's someone who still hasn't come out to their parents.

6.   No matter which profession you pursue, someone will always warn you about the danger of being perceived as "too gay." Take this advice very seriously, nod, and reply, "Darling, I hear you."

All the best,
*Old Paul*

# LINDA VILLAROSA

*Note to Self: May 1, 2011*
*Remember to ask Mom about The Terrible Day.*
*The Terrible Day so long ago is fixed in your memory. It haunts you,*
*but some of the details have faded. That's how you have dealt with it,*
*forgotten some of the hurt away.*

January 20, 1968, The Terrible Day
Dear Linda,

Your family is on the road, your favorite possessions with you in the car; the rest arriving in a big moving van a few days after you get to your new home. It's a real house, not an apartment. And you can't stop thinking about having your own room.

The trip from Chicago to Denver is two days long, and you are counting the seconds. Dad drives fast and hates to stop. He does slow down when your little sister gets carsick and throws up out the window. You roll yours down halfway and let the air blow through your fingers. You do the "toot toot" sign to a passing semi; the driver blasts his horn and smiles. You win the license plate game and wonder if you'll ever go to Maine or New York or Oregon. (You will.)

You can hardly stand it as your car pulls onto Pierce Street. It looks so clean. Mom sticks her head out the window and points. "There it is!" Your new home looks huge at the end of the block, bigger than in the black-and-white photo Dad took the day he and Mom walked around the neighborhood and then signed the papers. You ask, "Do we have to share it with another family?" Mom shakes her head no. Your sister asks, "Are we rich?" Everybody laughs.

Then you see it.

In chalk, the letters jagged and angry, somebody has written *Niggers Get Out* on your garage door and on the pavement on your driveway. It is meant to scare you. You are other. You are not like us. We hate you. Go back where you belong. You are not welcome.

Hard to imagine, but these days that word has lost much of its power. It's in songs that play on the radio. People use it casually, as an endearment. They soften the hard "er" with an "a." It's mostly "nigga" or the playful "niggaz" in plural. A man might call his friend "my nigga." A woman may say about her boyfriend, "that nigger is crazy."

You will find out who did it, Tim and Jim Hopkins*, the twins two doors down who deliver the paper. That same evening, your

*not their real rhyme-y names

doorbell will ring, and it'll be a white man collaring two sobbing bookend-brothers about your age. They will insist they did it on a dare. Their father will shake them down. Through tears, they'll say they're sorry. Their father will make them deliver the paper free for two months out of their allowance as penance.

Your family will have to live two doors down from theirs for years and years, until your parents sell the house. You'll go to all the same schools as Tim and Jim, who are a year ahead. You will blot them out of your mind, thinking only, "stupid, rhyme-y names" when you see them at school. You will later find Tim on Facebook (Lord, this is too complicated to explain; just wait and see what it is.). You feel a mean thrill when you see that he looks gray, overweight, and unhappy.

On the night of The Terrible Day, Mom will assure you that everything is fine. But something has changed for you. You understand that the world isn't kind. People you don't know will hate you for who you are.

As your mother explains to you and your sister, "No, don't worry. It was a mistake. The neighbors do want us here," you glance at your father's face, still tight with rage. You suspect what she's saying isn't true.

Tonight, you will sleep in your own room, but it won't feel as good as you thought it would. As your mom and dad kiss you good night and you snuggle into your new bed, you will understand that, no matter what, you will always have these three people who love you. It will always be the four of you. You are bound together by blood and love and pain and by the memory of The Terrible Day.

*April 30, 1979*

*Dear Linda,*

Y̶ou don't know it yet, but today is the day you're going to come out to your parents. It's not going to go well.

News flash: You're a lesbian! I'm giving you the information this way because you will also end up being a journalist. In this day and age, thirty-some years from right now, being a journalist is MUCH harder than being a lesbian! Trust me.

Anyway, it's really not news at all that you're a lesbian. You already know and everyone else suspects. That's why your mother and father are waiting to ambush you when you open the door to their bedroom and finally break the silence.

As unbelievable as it sounds, this whole coming out thing is going to work out fine. You're going to find the love of your life, a tall beautiful woman, who is kind and warm and Southern. She will whisper secrets to you in a voice that sounds like dessert.

You'll have two children. I know what you're thinking. But, yes, lesbians can have children. It's basic biology. You did well in high school science; you'll figure out how to make the kid thing happen.

Your children will call you "Mommy" even after they're too old for that corny sort of thing. The girl will be all arms, legs, and smiles. She'll be determined, a tough spirit, her brow furrowed on the day she is born. She's serious on the outside, with a soft, gooey center. When you look at your daughter, you'll see yourself.

Your son will be just soft and gooey. He'll take your hand when the two of you walk down the street, even though he's as tall as you. He'll be a good-time guy, who'll make you laugh until you can't catch your breath. Every time you look into his face, you'll see Dad.

But it doesn't feel that way today. Your home, in suburban Denver, will feel small and airless. Mom will ask, "Are you a lesbian?" She wants so badly for you to say no. But don't bother. She's as sure as first thing in the morning that it's true. You know her; she'll try and talk you out of it:

"Honey, you're not a lesbian."

"You might feel that way now, but it will go away and you'll be normal."

"No daughter of mine is a lesbian."

"We'll get you a good therapist."

"Why are you doing this to ME!?"

"You ARE not a lesbian!"

Dad won't say anything until the end. Then he'll tear up and whisper, "Do you hate men?"

I know you're afraid. You're scared that you will first lose your family and then, little by little, everybody else in your life. Especially every other black person. If the "community" — which means every black person you know, have ever met, or will meet — finds out you're a lesbian, THEY will take away your black card. And this is the "Say It Loud, I'm Black and I'm Proud" late '70s, a bad time to be black but not black — or black enough.

In your mind, you can't be black and gay. In the world you live in, all the gays are white, and all the blacks are straight. And in the big picture, you believe that being a lesbian is bad for the race. It might be good for you — but for twenty-nine million other people, it's bad bad bad. You're supposed to be a model, and do the right thing for the community, a race of people who have suffered so much.

But face it: Mostly you are terrified of a black community of only three. You are mostly afraid that your family will stop loving you when you admit that you're a lesbian. But they won't. The four of you are the lone survivors of The Terrible Day, and your shared history is a tie that binds you together.

You will reassure Dad that you don't hate men, especially not him. He will love you fiercely until his last breath, a shallow inhale that comes just hours before your son is born. Mom had no intention of pushing you away. After today, she will tighten her grip, pulling you closer . . . to torture you. She will continue to power away at you, doing everything she can to convince you that you are not a lesbian.

But you inherited her strength, her will, and that streak of stubbornness that runs right down your backbones. It will take her five years, but Mom will finally realize that she can't change you back. You will never be a proper black lady with good shoes and matching bag, who marries a professional African-American gentleman and has two kids. She will cut her losses and love her two grandbabies — and you.

One day many years later you will ask her if she wishes you were straight. She will hesitate, then say, "I love you just the way you are." You will never forget that.


Love,
*Linda*

# J. D. McClatchy

*Dear One,*

It's not that you're unrecognizable from here, but that it seems so long ago. History, lives, laws, attitudes have speeded up, but down that long corridor of change, there you are, nervously waiting to go onstage. It's 1963, senior year of high school, and you're starring in the school play, *Everyman*. That it was a medieval morality play, its hero torn by temptations and forced to choose between his good angel and his bad — well, it was the choice of the drama coach, the Jesuit who happened also to be my Greek teacher and for whose favor I longed. That *you* were Everyman is the irony, because in fact you were a peculiar, solitary, smart but unhappy individual, not at all like your classmates or contemporaries — or, for that matter, the character in the play. Eager to be an adult, you had loathed a childhood that enforced games and sports, rigid routines and conventions. You wanted to be "included," but kept yourself snobbishly apart. Rather than roughhouse with the boys, you preferred playing house with neighborhood girls. More than anything, you were bored.

But you had one advantage. You were gay from the start, and knew it. Your desires — no matter how troubling or temporarily confused — had a single, as yet unfocused, aim. You occasionally thought how, in the future, marriage or the priesthood might usefully hide those desires, but that was only because, as a teenager, everyone listens to what others say as a source of possibilities. One wants to fit in, wants to fulfill the expectations of the family, wants to succeed in society.

This was what they now call the Eisenhower Era — a term that might as well be the Dark Ages — a time of "soulless conformity." (Actually, the 1950s and early '60s were, as far as the arts were concerned, a period of innovation that can rival the 1920s.) It's often singled out as an especially horrid time to have been gay, enforcing a repressed or furtive life. A gay teenager seemed destined for marriage or suicide, and was raised amidst crushing social norms and religious bigotry.

And yet, you survived. The goals the age instilled in you, however twisted, were happiness and success — notions that are easy to scorn and hard to resist. And that, incredibly, was your fate as an adult. How come? There were dozens of reasons — luck, the right genes, good teachers, parents who blissfully ignored you. You didn't have any gay friends, or none that you knew of then, but you had what turned out to be a perfect guide: the Closet. In the age of enlightened responsibilities and openness, "the Closet" has almost as bad a reputation as the Eisenhower Era.

But you found a way to make a virtue out of its necessity.

By trying to pass as straight, by laughing at the wrong jokes, by muffling your advances, and by walking around with your head down, you learned a way of life that became invaluable to you as a writer. One of the first and most lasting lessons you eventually learned as a young writer — and it is impossible to separate this lesson from the fact you were gay — was lying, pretending. You learned to hide inside a pen. Or rather, the pen allowed you to learn the difference between *hiding* something and *disguising* something — that is to say, making it difficult but not impossible to see. A poem — and a person too? — needs disguises. It needs secrets. It thrives on the tension between what is said and not said; it prefers the oblique, the implied, the ironic, the suggestive; when it speaks, it wants a person to lean forward a little to overhear; it wants him to understand things only years later.

Of course, you didn't realize all that while you were standing in the wings, waiting for your cue to enter. (My first line was to be "Why asketh thou?") That was half a century ago. We all act. Some, alas, act out. If we're lucky, we learn to keep our private selves at a little remove, to savor them. And you were one of the lucky ones. In time, you learned not to fear but to appreciate the distance between the busy world and your secret, all the ramifications and delights you had in being you.


Love,


*Sandy*

# ANNE BOGART

*Dear Anne,*

I know, I know, you are driven by anger and revenge — anger against the circumstances of being brought up in a male-dominated Navy culture and revenge against what feels like an unending series of obstacles and rejections erected to annoy you and you alone. And I know that the energy produced by the anger and revenge is rich, useful, and seemingly limitless. Wonderful! Every adventure you have enjoyed, fueled by revenge and anger, led to voracious forages out into the wide world. And I know that the accumulating ambition and adventure led to insight, to travel, and to creative endeavor. All of this is true and wonderful. You used what was available to you — you made lemons into lemonade.

But how can I encourage you to listen far more closely to the subtle indications of your own body? How can I help you to trust the genius of your body and to move with more moment-to-moment responsiveness to the world and to follow the signals that your body is offering? If you listen closely, the body will let you know who and what to trust and who and what to avoid. The mind, though, which is the wiliest part of your body, will trick you. The prefrontal cortex of your brain makes you prejudiced and frightened and you second-guess your instincts. Subsequently you power through things too much. But please know that it is possible to savor the moments and drink in the sensations that wash over you as a direct result of your efforts in the world, whatever your efforts are, including the creation of plays, which is what you always seem to gravitate toward. Taste and revel in these moments because they will mitigate your fear and give you the feedback that you need to move forward gracefully. The moment-to-moment sensations of the body do not lie. Use your body as a barometer. Trust the goose bump factor. When someone, or something, gives you goose bumps — or as the French call it far more poetically, *frisson de corps* — pay attention. Locate the source of this physical excitement and then follow the ensuing cues, whether they indicate initiating a new relationship or diving into a new play. Your body is telling you something. Trust these indications and your sense of adventure. I am suffering now as a direct result of your lack of sensitivity to the indications of your body. You pushed too hard. You did not trust your instincts and you did not trust the other bodies around you. You need to understand that, like cattle, we are a species that herds. We move through life in relation to others — in relation to other people's bodies. Try to make choices in the moment by trusting the body — your body and the bodies around you. Today the ache in my hips is a constant reminder of your willful excesses and abuses. Did you mean to hurt me? Did you think about me at all?

I am thinking of you now with sympathy for your churning stomach and your constant sense of inadequacy and doubt that plagues you each step of the way. Oh, I know now that you do not in fact have to prove yourself with every step that you take. Can't you see that like-minded friends and colleagues around you will help, will come to your rescue, will join with you and together you will make it to the next clearing? How can I encourage you to trust your body and the bodies of those around you in the moment-to-moment unfolding of your life and the lives of those around you? As Aristotle said, we find meaning in relation to those around us. I am aware now that what you do with your body and how you move through the world matters. You carry it all with you, through time, in the body. You are speaking to me now and every day. I carry you with me.

Yours always,

*Anne*

# ERIC ORNER

YOU DON'T YET KNOW THAT FOR A LITTLE WHILE YOU'LL GET PAID TO DRAW CARTOONS FOR THE WORLD'S MOST FAMOUS MOUSE, OR THAT, ONCE THE LITTLE WHILE IS OVER, YOU WON'T WIND UP MISSING HIM VERY MUCH...

THAT TINKER BELL TRULY SUCKS...

YOU'RE FIRED!

ERIC O.

SOME GUY ON THE GYMNASTICS TEAM @ A HIGH SCHOOL THREE TOWNS OVER...

YOU DON'T YET KNOW THAT ONE OF THE CUTEST JOCKS IN HIGH SCHOOL IS GAY, AND WOULD ALSO END UP A GREAT FRIEND DESPITE NEVER SPEAKING A WORD TO YOU BACK WHEN YOU WERE BOTH TEENAGERS...

AND YOU DON'T YET KNOW THAT YOU'LL BE LUCKY ENOUGH TO SPEND THE NEXT 30 YEARS GRATEFUL FOR THE COMPANY OF YOUR MOM, BROTHER, STEPDAD, NIECE AND NEPHEW... AND THAT YOU'LL EVEN SORTA COME TO ENJOY YOUR FATHER...

YOU DON'T KNOW YOU'LL FALL IN LOVE. YOU DON'T KNOW THAT SOMEONE WILL FALL IN LOVE WITH YOU BACK.

YOU DON'T KNOW A LOT... YOU'LL FIND OUT. IT WILL BE WORTH IT...

116

# LUCY JANE BLEDSOE

*Dear Little Lucy,*

Good news! You were right. About everything. Every last thing.

Okay, maybe not every word that came out of your mouth needed to be said. Maybe you exaggerated a bit — often and a lot? — because you were afraid of not being heard. Maybe you sometimes told lies because you needed to hear the words out loud to know that they weren't true.

But those slips, those tiny tests, those moments where you cut yourself in half, or maybe into many pieces, to experiment with truth, aren't what I'm talking about. I'm talking about what you knew, in your core, to be true.

You were right.

Think about it.

There you are at age twelve, an oversized girl in tights and a leotard, clumping across the wooden ballet studio. Skinny Mrs. Shoemacher, with her hair pulled into a tight bun, slapping out the rhythm with her hands. You wanted the tutu. You wanted to feel how your body could move. You wanted your older sister to like you. You wanted grace. Nothing wrong with tutus, movement, your sister, and grace. But ballet? You hated it. *Hated* it.

Now compare that with sitting at the long dinner table at summer camp with Miss Jo at the head. You loved her unfashionably short hair. You loved how loudly she sang. You loved the goofy faces she made. You loved the way she bumped hips with other counselors. You even loved the attention when she asked, "What are you looking at?" if you stared at her for too long. You knew that Miss Jo was one of the most genuine people you'd ever met. You knew, back then when you were just twelve years old, that you belonged at her dinner table and not in Mrs. Shoemacher's ballet studio.

Getting to right, knowing what is true for you, was the hard part. It still is. Wouldn't it be nice to be able to go online, pull up a search engine, and type in: *true, Lucy, now.*

What you did took a bit more time. It involved running away and digging giant holes in the earth. Even theft and arson. It seemed like you were committing random acts of destruction. But even then you were working your way toward the life you needed. You were building forts that kept you safe and nurtured your imagination.

*Fort #1:* You are five years old. You have two older brothers and an older sister. They're playing baseball and running track, fine-tuning their fashion statements and making friends with other kids. Who are you? You're not sure. You find an opening in the bushes at the side of the house. You crawl in and find a hefty branch that holds your weight. When you sit there, you are all alone. No one knows where you are. No one knows *who* you are. It is the perfect fort, with the walls of green leaves and chairs of bouncy branches. You realize that when you go into your fort, maybe with some cookies or a book, you are just you. You realize that it feels very, very good to be you, alone, your five-year-old self emerging into a girl who loves green.

*Fort #2:* You are ten years old. You and your best friend, Michelle, like to play girl and boy. You like to make out. You especially like to do this when you construct an elaborate story to hold the play. You are a basketball star and she is a cheerleader. She is a park ranger and you are a tourist. You are a photographer and she is your model. You both are explorers, working your way up the wilds of a previously unknown river.

Her father catches you in the tent in the backyard. You both have your shirts off. She's lying on top of you and you're making out. He tells you to never do that again.

That's when you built the next fort. There is a vacant lot up the street, and you decide you'll build a dugout house, like the ones in Laura Ingalls Wilder's books. You spend an entire September digging the hole, arguing about how far down you have to go before angling horizontal to the surface to make the "room." You want to put an armchair down there, and also a shelf to hold your box of cookies and books.

Unfortunately, a construction crew arrives and begins digging their own hole for a new house. You have to abandon that fort.

*Fort #3:* The following summer, however, the house hasn't been finished. The construction site is fun to explore in the evenings, after the crew goes home. Sometimes you pee in the room that will eventually become the bathroom. You put loose nails in your pockets. This gives you an idea.

Not far away is a patch of woods. Everyone calls it Pete's Woods because mean Mr. Peterson has the only house in the dark forest. You and Michelle begin stealing scrap lumber from the construction site and dragging it to your own construction site in the woods. You select a nice muddy spot right by the creek. That way you'll have water for drinking and washing. You use the nails you've collected in your pockets and a hammer you take from your family's garage. You manage to get the floor and two walls up before the fire.

You don't light the match. But you sure don't stop Jeff, a neighbor boy, from lighting it. You're fascinated by the way he knows how to gather a ball of pitch from the tree, place it in a nest of paper scraps. The fire flares up as a group of kids stand by and watch. You know you should stop this from happening. Instead, once the fire is real, engulfing the tree, soon to jump onto your half-built fort, you run. You never find out who called the fire department. You stand with the other neighbors at a distance and watch the firefighters stretch their hoses into the woods. Everyone hates Mr. Peterson, but no one wants his house to burn down. It is an awful moment, and you feel a hefty responsibility.

The firefighters manage to put out the fire. You and Michelle abandon that fort.

*Fort #4:* Your last fort is the most elaborate of them all. It exists only in your imagination. You are thirteen years old. You've quit those ballet lessons. Michelle has moved to Canby, Oregon. You are actively trying to sort out what kind of girl and woman you want to be. Nothing that you see around you fits the bill.

So you and your best friend, Shannon, come up with what you called Our Plan, or OP for short. In the near future you are going to run away. You spend time in the garage stockpiling sleeping bags and a tent, canned foods and reading material. You study maps and select Duniway Park. Not only does it have lots of shrubbery and trees for cover, it's located near downtown for easy access to stores. Each week driving to church, piled with your siblings in the family station wagon, you pass Duniway Park. You always study the landscape, looking for the perfect tree under which — maybe even *in* which — to set up camp. You and Shannon make maps, draw plans for the campsite, and keep notes on how exactly you will survive.

When you finally do run away, you haven't yet set up the camp and so you have nowhere to go. Several hours later, you're forced to return home.

You never quite finished building any of your forts. But I know what you were doing. You were constructing safety. Places where you could sort out who you were. Places where you could be somebody very different from all the other somebodies in your life. Sitting in all your forts, from the found one in the bushes to the half-constructed ones deep in the earth or in the woods or in written plans, you also knew that you loved your body. You loved the way it moved, the way it absorbed food, the way it felt a deep pleasure in nature. The forts housed your love for trees and animals, your need for privacy, your deep, deep knowledge that you did know what is true for you. The forts housed your imagination too, the stories you wanted to someday tell.

I'm much older now, but I'm still building forts. I call them novels. I build stories to house the dreams, mishaps, loves, and shenanigans of people I want to have around. A good novel, like a good fort, houses what is true.

So that's the good news. You don't have to have courage. You don't have to fight or change anyone. You just have to know what's true. Trees. Friends. Singing. Love. Stories. And you already know that.

Love,

*Big Lucy*

# TONY VALENZUELA

*Dear Toto,*

I know you're worried now that you've entered ninth grade and still don't feel like you belong. For a long time, you've understood that you're not a boy like most of the boys in school (except for always-in-trouble Herbie, you'll see), not like your brothers or cousins or any of your sister's boyfriends (except Amir, she'll see). I know you don't feel like a *normal boy*. You never have. You hate to fight and you don't get baseball. You like to be friends with girls, but that's all. You don't even feel very American, having grown up in Guadalajara. In fact, the only boys you like to be around are your Mexican cousins (this will change) because they look up to you. The boys at school only seem to want to play sports or play rough (this won't).

Toto, feeling like you belong is never going to be easy for you. I'm writing to you from your older self to share a little advice.

Those urges you're having about Coach Pugmire (though you dread PE) and Mr. Boswell from World History class (which you love) — you're afraid they aren't *normal* feelings. (By the way, one day, I promise, you will actually like to exercise, and you'll never forget *sapere aude* from Mr. Boswell's class: "dare to know.") You've been hiding these urges about these teachers and about some of the boys at school because you think they're wrong. Everybody says they're wrong, in so many words. You even prayed for them to go away but they haven't.

Especially now, since watching those two men kiss in that movie on Showtime while locked in your bedroom (even though Kate Jackson from *Charlie's Angels* was the star, it was still R-rated and you couldn't risk anyone walking in) — you're absolutely certain you're not like other boys. *Not normal.* There they were on television, two *handsome* men kissing as passionately as Jeff and Fallon on *Dynasty*! You had never seen two men kiss before. It made you shake inside and feel weak and out of breath, like when Coach Pugmire makes your PE class run around the field. Your knees were wobbly and your heart was pounding. When the movie was over, you went to the bathroom and stared at yourself in the mirror for a long time like you didn't recognize the person in it, as if this was the very first time you saw yourself. I remember what you whispered very quietly: *"I'm one of them."*

Toto, the first thing I want to tell you is that being one of them will someday feel like a gift more special and luxurious than that angora sweater Mom and Dad bought you. Whatever anguish you're experiencing now about these urges will eventually disappear and you'll feel as right as you've ever felt, as if granted by one of Mrs. Templeton's permission slips. And then, one day, in about four years, you're going to experience your own real kiss for the first time. You'll be on a date with a guy from Switzerland (really!). He will seem different from anyone you've ever met but wonderful with his golden hair and thick accent. It'll happen after dinner as you walk out of the restaurant onto the crowded street. Before saying good night he'll lean in to kiss you but you'll flinch your head back, startled. He'll whisper, "It's okay. This is West Hollywood," and those words will sound like a revelation. That's all you'll need to hear! You'll let him kiss you on the lips without paying attention to the people around you, *as if it were normal*, two young men kissing on the sidewalk in public in full view of traffic chugging along the avenue.

Toto, you're going to feel a lot of pressure from kids (and adults!) to be normal. But you'll never feel normal when by "normal" you know that people mean "like everybody else."

Your family is not normal. They're Mexican *and* Italian and different than all of your friends' families. Growing up in Mexico isn't normal, not to the kids at school who sometimes say awful things you can't believe they mean ("You're not *Mexican*-Mexican," one of the girls said to you once without blinking, as if that was supposed to be a compliment). But you already know a lot more about the world than they do, that there's a whole universe outside of El Cajon, California. When Mom made that entire tray of *pollo con mole* for you to take to the school banquet back in the sixth grade, you fretted that she hadn't made enough. But not a single kid tried it, not even one of your teachers, and you brought the whole tray back home (which Aunt Chagua was happy about).

To the kids at school, eating *mole* wasn't normal. So then who wants to be normal?

Here's the most important thing I need to tell you, Toto. Don't ever confuse "normal" with "better." People will confuse the two your entire life (*especially* adults) but they're wrong. Being different (some people will say "weird" but, remember, they're just boring) is going to bring you thrills and great adventure. Being "one of them" will make your life interesting, different, unique, and you'll wonder, *Why was I ever worried about being normal?*

Love,

*Tony*

# CAROLE DeSANTI

*Dear Carole,*

I want to talk to you about Sanibel Island, Florida. I hear it's still a beautiful spot: wild and lush and a world away from everything — the perfect escape. Perfect for a plan dreamed up in the backseat of that old Dodge, Dad driving due south, fleeing the frigid Lake Erie winds, the Ohio-gray sky — Mom on the passenger side, busy with the maps.

The whole family drove down together right after Christmas that year. As we passed through West Virginia, the Carolinas, and down through Georgia, the weather got sunnier and warmer; pretty soon we were looking at oranges growing on trees, real palm trees, and an azure sky. It was a minor miracle — vacation — a real one, with a beach. For once, everyone was happy.

Kind of a mess, now, isn't it.

You needed to reinvent yourself, you thought, wedged into the backseat with your two brothers, one still in a baby seat. You

127

needed something to help you stand up to those locker room girls back home — the magazine-reading, gum-smacking, cigarettes-in-the-john taunters with their mascara wands and their ice-blue eyelids. And — especially — for *her*. Your ex–best friend with her exacting standards for how feet should look in sandals, or breasts in halter tops, along with benchmarks for appropriate progress in the boyfriend-area. ("That top looks too slutty! And your heels are the wrong shape. They shouldn't go out in a bump but down smoothly like this, see?") Her mom bought her halter top in an expensive department store, and it was a different kind of garment altogether — it looked like a costume from *South Pacific*. And there was nothing at all to be done about your feet.

Mom — looking deceptively benign up there in the front seat — has gone from bad to worse recently, prohibiting halter tops of any kind, as well as short skirts, platform shoes, tight jeans, and even tank tops. You've been stashing away money from baby-sitting and sneaking out to stores. How did the other girls control their mothers? Maybe they didn't have to. Anyway, the scrap of blue polyester that was your new halter top didn't pass muster with your friend either. Maybe it could pass as half a bathing suit in Florida. Mom might buy that.

And once you got to Sanibel, there he was, your dream come true: cute, older — seventeen, he said — tough-looking with dirty blond hair down to his tan shoulders (no shirt), jeans. It was cool, walking down the beach with him, with the sea right there, and the palm trees. You'd been tanning with baby oil, and wearing that halter with cutoffs. In Florida it fit right in. He slipped his arm around your shoulders on the beach, held your hand for a while — it felt wild and free, dangerous, thrilling, dizzying as the sun, after a day lying out, listening to the surf. You'd never even made out with a guy, and it was high time to fix that. Maybe he'd give you a photograph to take back home. That's about as far as your thinking went.

It didn't play out that way, though, did it?

I know. You're shit-scared. And it's hard to think straight, because all of that baby-oil tanning came out in blisters, a rash all over your body, and a fever. Sun poisoning. That giddy feeling felt great, while the waves were crashing. And then it didn't.

Here's the Kleenex box. I'm sorry; so sorry. And I have to tell you that you're right about a few things. One is that telling Mom and Dad, which you will have to do because they'll drag it out of you, is only going to make it worse. I wish I could go back and redo that scene, inject some kindness into it.

OK. Let's go over it in detail. Not just what happened — what led up to it, the whole tumbling mess of thoughts and feelings that led up to this jam. Because things have to change, right? They've changed already.

First, home. The Florida trip aside, it's pretty bad, not that you know exactly what's going on. Mom and Dad say you're too young to understand, but still they seem to be turning to you to take care of them and fix things. How can you fix them if you don't know what they are? *Do the dishes,* Mom says. *Scrub the tub. Change the baby.* But these tasks, aside from being tedious, solve zero problems, zilch. Mom and Dad are holding the reins and driving everyone off the cliff, yelling and screaming the whole way. All through this year, you feel like you'd been asleep in the back of the wagon (like Laura in *Little House on the Prairie*) and woke up in the middle of a disaster. You can see it so much more clearly now. That's been the net result of being fourteen.

Your best friend changed too. No more long talks, sleepovers, and secrets. Now, it's only about boys, clothes you can't afford, and full-body critiques in front of the mirror. Those boys at school . . . there's not a decent prospect in the bunch, but somehow, she finds guys to cultivate. Her idea is to find a boyfriend at a lower rung on the popularity ladder, but still acceptable, then hang around with him and his friends and work her way up. She ranks them all, according to a system. Where did this technique come from? One day, she just announced it. The idea you put forward (tentatively, in the face of her master plan) was that you should at least like the person, first — his personality or something about him, *anything.* She got rid of that idea. Totally the wrong way to go about it, she said. And there she went. She has a new best girlfriend now too, one who lives in a neighborhood conveniently close to the current target guy.

It's lonely without her, that's what hurts. She was the smart, funny friend who dreamed up adventures like no one else, who read books and told stories, who understood everything without any need for explanations. Now there's a big blank space where she was, a gap in your life.

Between her new ideas, though, and Mom's out-of-date ones, it's like being drawn and quartered. It's all about to explode and it may as well. So, Florida. Cue the palm trees and the breeze and the baby oil, and a guy who had it all over any of those jerks at school. Even she would have to admit he was a total coup. You'd need a photo, though. She'd never believe you otherwise.

As luck would have it, Mom and Dad were so happy on Sanibel that they decided to buy a few more nights at the hotel. Another miracle. And the sun had done its magic; you were tan, and rosy, with a feverish feeling that the world was tipping and you could almost fall off, shake off everything about the old life and become one with the beach, the gulls and sandpipers, oranges from the trees, and a guy's tan hand holding yours.

A bunch of girls had planned a big pool party for the last night. The halter was again deployed. Things got a little rowdy at the pool, with a gaggle of girls, the beach-guy and his friend, who was bigger, older, and not so cool looking. You all pretty much took over the place, for an underwater treasure hunt or something. I don't remember — some game. In the midst of this you discovered the strings on the halter top had suddenly been untied — his uncouth friend was responsible, not him — and there you were, bare on top, and surprised, a little freaked out but everyone was laughing and having a good time, so it wasn't such a big deal. But Mom must have been watching from the balcony because before you could even get that thing tied back up she was yanking you out of that pool by the arm, breaking up the party. *Humiliation.*

The sun poisoning was beginning to kick in, though. You took a lot of aspirins, and the combination numbed you out to the worst of her yelling.

The next day — the last day — he told you to meet him, not on the beach but in a part of the hotel that was vacant, about to be cleaned by the maids. He even might've said he wanted to apologize, just hang out before your family left. But when you met him there, it all happened so fast. Way too fast.

OK, I won't go into the gory details; we both remember them well enough. He didn't care about hanging out, talking, whatever. He got you down on the bed — *hey, wait a minute!* But he didn't. Pinned you down on someone else's dirty sheets with an ashtray of butts on the table next to it. It all happened in an instant. But he must have planned it.

You got out. Belted out a scream and bolted, as soon as you could get him off you. Not quite soon enough.

OK — another tissue. Don't worry, we have a full box.

I can tell you, now — you're not irrevocably harmed. You're not pregnant, and you don't have a venereal disease — these are the kinds of things Mom is obsessed with, and punishing you for — for the possibility of either — although, either would be punishment enough. Yes, they are concerns, but what has really hurt you is something else, something she doesn't see. It's gotten pushed to the background because fending off Mom and Dad has taken precedence, now, over what was wrong to begin with.

How could he have treated you like that, all of a sudden? The *simpático* of the beach — the talking, laughing, joking around with everyone — that was gone. It had all been a lie, an act, a feverish mirage. In that room you were no longer yourself but someone else, *who did he think you were?* He snapped his fingers and turned you into a non-person, not-yourself, with no say about what was going to happen. A thing. That's what it was like. It was what you had always been afraid death would be like. Just — not-being.

Now, all you want to do is get past it. Forget it as quickly as possible and get Mom and Dad off your back. But, you had a role in what happened, and that must be looked at — through your own eyes, not your best friend's, not your mother's. What you really felt, on the beach, even: that you were swimming out beyond your depth. In fact, you were breaking your own rule: that you needed to like something about him, first. Aside from the way he looked, which, mainly, was how he'd look *to her.* To the others back at school.

What he did was wrong (that fact, in all of the blame you're putting on yourself, seems to have gotten lost). But, now you know there is something more important than living out someone else's story, or even one you invent. It is something that you must take more care to guard. You must stand as gatekeeper to the realm of the not-you. To places you don't belong, people to whom you don't belong. To what can hurt you even as you go out to explore the world.

The shape of your own life is coming into view. In a very short time, it will begin to emerge. And it's better than a few palm trees and a guy on a beach. But, you must guard its promise.

The world is larger than it seems. I know you think you can imagine it — from books, TV — the Departures board at Cleveland Hopkins, where you can stare up and contemplate escaping to Chicago or New York. In fact, there are lakes in Switzerland clearer than any picture; mountains and fjords in Norway that will take your breath away; steaming-hot rivers with healing powers in Mexico; and hilltops in France where the sun sets and the moon rises at once. In London, you will wander down Shakespeare's streets and read books in a library built like an enormous ship. In a few years, some good luck will come your way. All of this will come about, though, because of the way you are going to take hold of things right now, and begin to steer your own passage. Now, it's only in books that you read about lives others are allowed to live, the places they can go. But soon, stories will weave in and out of life — a life that belongs to you and no one else. Love will come into it too — and it will be true love, even though at the moment, reassurance on this point is thin.

What? Oh, I get it — let's get going! Let's be there, already — there and not here. It's all taking way too long and it's miserable.

Well, I have to say something about that. As it's going to be a dilemma for years to come, I'd love to save us both some trouble.

It's about time. Time is not numbers on a clock, it is not a countdown to Christmas or summer vacation — or the months or years until you're allowed to drink, drive, or get out. Now, time seems to take forever. Even later, you're going to be hopping mad and impatient with many, many things. But, actually, time and the way it unfolds has better ideas for your life than you do. Life has its own plan, and time is the language it speaks. Right now it's a foreign tongue, like French, only there are no classes in it. In your case (it works differently for everyone) time is more your friend than you know. It will show you how to trust your perceptions. The more you tune in to what you sense and feel, and test it over time, the more quickly things will change for the better.

For now, it's absolutely fine not to like ice-blue eye shadow, the way nail polish suffocates your nails, and the guys at school. Don't bother about finding a solution to the halter-top crisis. In fact, the gigantic fight about what your body should look like and what it should and shouldn't do is going to get worked out very soon. Your true instincts — once all of the static and noise is banished — are the best guides.

As far as Mom and Dad go, they are pretty upset right now. They aren't able to make very good use of their love for you, but it's not that they don't love and care for you. They can't remember what it's like to be fourteen, and they are in the throes of their own problems. They are going to have to pull themselves through, just as you need to pull yourself through yours. Just love them as much as you can, when you can, and keep focused on what you need to do: work hard, and learn.

The last thing I'd like to tell you, and I know this is hard, is to let your friend go without all the envy, blame, and hurt; without trying to turn back the clock. Let her slip away. She needs to go. She's going to do a lot of things, and have a lot of things that you're going to wish you had, for a while. But you are going to find your way, as well. Eventually, one day, she will reappear. She's going to get in touch when you least expect it, and you'll talk it over in detail, what happened between the two of you.

These lessons will take a while to sink in. But I thought I'd plant the seed. Meanwhile, no more baby-oil tanning, OK? Use sunscreen. I, your future self, will thank you.

Love,

*Carole*

# GREGORY MAGUIRE

*Dear G,*

Hey, put down the library book. (What is it, anyway? Oh, *Grimm's Fairy Tales*? Again? Aren't you a little old for that?)

Just kidding! It's me. Yeah, you, but as me. Later. Hailing you from the Great Dim Distance of the Middle Ages — your Middle Ages. (The next century, can you believe it?) I'm writing to tell you one or two things I think you would want to know, back when you are a boy, roughly between the ages of losing your grade school milk money, on the one hand, and finding yourself a glass of very pink wine in a plastic cup with the college seal on it, on the other.

Here's the thing that will surprise you. (Not *may* surprise you, but *will*, because I know that at thirteen and fifteen and seventeen you worry otherwise.)

*The things you most enjoy about being a kid do not evaporate as you age.*

True, other things happen to you, in time. Other anxieties heave onto the horizon. Other woes squat like a heat inversion over your life and refuse to budge. And other pleasures and satisfactions captivate (far more rewardingly than you can imagine). Certain capacities emerge, like a penchant for hard thinking, a talent that you lust for more than you lust for romance. (And at fifteen, as I remember, mostly you don't lust for romance, yet. You don't lurk for it and you hardly even look for it, because you aren't really sure where to look yet.)

But the private boyishness that fits on you like a second skin — like your first skin — you don't shed it as you grow up (no matter what today's mirrors show).

You worry that if you turn out to be, um, gay — or gay-ish — you will have to change. Toughen up. Laugh cynically and blow smoke rings in the face of optimism and good cheer. Laugh with a smoker's laugh, bitter at life. Don't deny it, you worry. I know you do.

I remember you so well. I know you don't practice the words for who you are or how you are, but you suspect you are . . . um. Different. *Sensitif.* Alert. Comic. Polite. Drawn to the mystery and rituals of faith and to the consolations of music and to the infinite purities of poetry. You're adroit and sometimes almost clever. (You don't yet know you are also brave, but come on: Being able to know all the above about yourself, as a boy, and not collapse or Go Over to the Jock Side — that means you're brave.)

Also you're so earnest that it's embarrassing, even to yourself too, but you have made a promise, almost in infancy it seems, not to lie about yourself. Not to Give In. And saying things directly is important to you — maybe because that Irish-Catholic midcentury culture of your earliest years, however celebratory of storytelling it is, shies away from the immodest discussion of the deeper feelings.

None of these attributes of yours will change. The ninth-grade kid who stops at a curb and squats to root through his knapsack for a journal to write down something — I'm still you. The tenth-grade kid who, in a crowd, finds his Own Kind (and here I don't mean gay, necessarily) by seeing whose faces light up when the subject of good books arises, and what good books suggest — that's still you. I'm still you. The high school junior who secretly doesn't wear undershirts because he likes how the worn teal-blue-with-cranberry-stripe plaid flannel shirt from the Army Navy shop pulls softly against the skin of his back and arms — I'm still you.

And — yes, as it happens — the boy who can be suffused with an interior sting of pleasure at the sight of a sweet male friend, that seltzery surge you thought was perhaps a complaint of the intestines or a deformity of character — that's still you too. You don't lose that. You don't outgrow it. It's not Just a Phase.

You worry that like those babies in *Mary Poppins* who in growing up couldn't talk to the birds anymore, like Wendy in *Peter Pan* who became too old to fly, you will have to grow too old to be your natural, true self too. Stop being a Lost Boy, settle for being a dwarf pirate, maybe Smee.

But the tender sort of lostness of not yet being sure, a lostness that makes you alert and capable and even skilled at imagining yourself in other people's skins to see what makes them tick — you get to keep that useful, vital lostness.

Yes, of course, you do grow and mature. You fall in love. You manage to seem even a little dignified. (Gravitas has to stand in for cute, after a while. It's a bummer.) But the boy in the plaid flannel shirt still lives in your skin when you go to bed and when you get up, when you stand at a podium to make a speech or console your kids or kiss your beloved husband or return to your house in France or sing at church or read poetry with your dearest old friends or autograph your books at a festival.

(Oh, sorry. I wasn't going to tell you about any of that. YES! You actually get to be PUBLISHED! And you get to be friends with some of your HEROES! Like oh not to name names but like MAURICE SENDAK! I know! I KNOW! SCREAMMM! And that's just the start of it! But I promised I wouldn't give away the plot.)

You have a better handle on the program than you think, though you consider yourself . . . well, not so much faggy, because you don't really get what that means yet (I won't be cruel and tell you how long you'll have to wait). You just think of yourself as sort of . . . loose. Open. Apprehensive, in the way that means "trying to apprehend, to unriddle some of this." Somewhat sui generis ("all in your own category"). You use your journal to do it (and I still keep them. I'm on Volume 57). You're telling me who *I'm* going to be, and I'm still listening.

Just one thing, though.

Feeling a little different, even unique, you too glibly assume that your task of being true to yourself is unprecedented in human history. It's easy (and sometimes fun) to wallow in the sadness of being separate because it makes you seem that much more richly individual.

If you can, try not to succumb to the narcissism of loneliness too much. Mind you take care of someone else while you're taking care of yourself. We all are struggling to release our souls from stone, like those sculptures of Michelangelo you will come to love. Each person doesn't turn out the same, of course, but we are all equally different. Go back and reread *Harriet the Spy* and concentrate on how Harriet finally apprehends — unriddles — Sport and Janie at the end. And how that apprehension finishes the job of making her a real writer.

(And YES! I still love *Harriet the Spy*! I read it EVERY YEAR! SCREAMMM! There's still NOTHING BETTER! I know, I KNOW!!!)

As ever,

*G*

# CHRISTOPHER RICE

*Dear Christopher,*

People will tell you to take yourself less seriously. You will think they're trying to dismiss you, that they are no different from the teachers who admonished you for being too sensitive, too eccentric, too unlike the other kids. But that's not the case. They're asking you to judge yourself by what you *do*, and not by what you think and feel. Because what you think and feel is always going to be a little bit *off*. That's just who you are. You think every birthmark might be cancerous, you fear every relationship will end with some soap operatic betrayal. Don't worry so much. Bad things *will* happen, but not the ones you've chosen to worry about in advance.

Your way in the world will be determined by how you *respond* to what happens to you, not by what happens to you, or your thoughts or feelings about it. This is the measure of a human being, and this will build self-esteem, enough self-esteem to overcome all the moments when jocks coughed the word *faggot* into their fists as you walked past, just because you loved theater and you turned in English assignments on bright red printer paper.

Good for you for coming out when you did. (Although, to be honest, eighteen doesn't seem so young anymore.) But I'd like to save you the time you're going to waste trying to become a more *acceptable* homosexual, by landing a partner you're sure will impress your straight friends and family members, by remaking yourself into a fashion plate or a bitter sophisticate or a pretend jock or a carefree party boy. And I wish I could keep you away from the endless party that is gay nightlife, that always moving train of music, dancing, and drugs that will promise you everything and deliver nothing. For some of us, especially someone with your emotional sensitivity, someone who has a dozen critical voices running in his head at all times, this world of instant gratification can become self-destructive to the point of being deadly. I pray that you make it through this part alive, with nothing more terminal than a few scars you learn from. The best way to do this? Treat others as you would like to be treated. Don't wear your feelings on your sleeve because you want someone to fix them for you. Hold the door open for the lady behind you at Starbucks. Be the polite stranger you would like to run into on the street. The ripple effects of these seemingly mundane actions will be vast, I promise you.

None of this will be easy, admitting that even after coming out, you're still hamstrung by an old, persistent desire to be accepted by those who don't (and may not ever) accept you. On some days, self-awareness can feel like guzzling sand. But it only *feels* that way, and those painful moments are often followed by great freedom. It's distracting and exhausting, keeping track of all the different masks you use to fit yourself into social situations that don't nurture who you are. Once you put them aside, you'll discover you care more about geeky airplane trivia than high fashion, that books make for better companions than pills. You'll begin to build a life that feeds your soul instead of attacking it. I wish such a life for you. You deserve one. We all do.

I know it's a lot to keep track of. Maybe it wasn't a good idea to tell you this all in one big burst. And you can't learn it all at once. (I'm still learning it.) It won't be what you expect and it may not always be what you want, but it will always be worth living for.

I Love You,


*Christopher*

# JEWELLE GOMEZ

*Hi,*

I know ten-year-olds hate when adults tell them, "It will all be fine!" But I was just looking at that picture of you at your tap-dancing recital and had to say a couple of things. In the picture you're wearing that cute little short costume. It was red, white, and blue and you're saluting the camera. Despite the military overtones of the costume I love that photograph of you.

But, I finally figured out why you never liked it — you think you look fat. You are so wrong! I know what it's like being stuffed into some outfit, and they never make things the right size. But that's them being wrong, not you.

Don't let anyone — movie stars, TV, advertisers, whatever — short-circuit your sense of your own beauty! Why is only size 0 a good thing? And, anyway, looking like everybody else makes it impossible to be picked out of a crowd. Who needs that?

Just between us, I'll tell you a secret . . . about thirty years from now you'll marry the girl of your dreams (butch with red hair), honest, but I won't give away her name. One day she and a friend will have a moment of silence in honor of the beauty of your thighs, I swear!

And about hair. There's no such thing as good hair or bad hair. There's only hair and no hair. So let that hang-up go too.

You probably don't get it yet, but you are a lesbian feminist femme, which is a lot of fun. You'll be deeply involved with politics and people and makeup. Most of the time you won't feel lonely like you do now because there's always a potluck supper, a poetry reading, or a meeting to go to. (Just kidding about the potluck.)

A few more things: Sex is good, which is another thing the faceless mob would like to convince you is not true. You get to decide about your sex life and you can have it any way you like it. You'll know what I'm talking about later, just remember the idea of Howard Johnson's 28 flavors when the sex debate comes up.

I know that the Civil Rights Movement has really heightened your awareness of the politics of being who you are, even as a kid. It feels exciting, like the world is on the brink of change. Well, yes and no. There is no brink of change. Change is not a cliff you jump off of or a doorway you pass through. There's a stream of change and we're always in it whether we notice or not. Being a lesbian feminist means you'll get to help steer through and shape the change like those people you see marching on TV on the six o'clock news. So jump in, the water's tumultuous and always will be.

Finally, you're a colored, lesbian, feminist writer — sorry, nothing to be done about that. This may be a lot for a ten-year-old to take in, so just breathe. First, the bad news: The mainstream publishing world will always marginalize you because it thinks no one cares what women of color have to say.

Now, the good news: If you care passionately about what we have to say, you'll love to write no matter how marginalized you might be, and you won't be alone out there on the margins.

There's something compelling about that photo; you put on a public smile like the photographer told you to, even though you hated being so exposed. That bravura will serve you well and that picture is actually you saluting yourself.

Maybe you should think about writing vampire stories, they might come back into fashion someday.

Love,

*Jewelle*

# BILL CLEGG

*Dear Billy,*

Are you twelve? Thirteen? Or younger — eight? Nine? I can't remember when it was that you first thought dying was the answer. The more I think about it, the more I remember, I think, actually, you were six or seven. Oh, Billy. I wish I were nearby to slap your back and tell you you're a good kid, that the bus won't flip like you pray it will, the plane won't crash, and the bolt of lightning won't come and deliver you from all those fearful hours. You'll find other things to deliver you from the feelings you fear, and as much as I wish you wouldn't, I know you have to. But the most important thing is that you'll live. So much longer than you ever imagined. Don't panic about that part; it turns out okay. I know you won't believe this, but it does all turn out okay. Better than okay. I won't spoil anything — you'll have to go through it all, every last minute of it, because as a friend of yours will tell you gently one particularly difficult day — *we can only learn at the speed of pain.* What I can say is that there will be some magnificent moments and there will also be some that don't seem survivable. But don't spend so much time thinking about the future. It's going to happen no matter how much you worry about it. And it won't be anything like you imagine. It will be harder, easier, more bewildering, and a million times more joyful than you expect. And, eventually, beyond your wildest dreams.

Okay, I'll spoil one thing. Even though I know you won't believe me, I'll tell you this one thing because maybe it will make the next years a little less hopeless. This is the thing: You'll love Dad. You'll look to him for advice and support and there will be times when he is the only person you think you can call. He will be there for you. He will tell you he loves you and that he's proud of you. And all this will happen after he knows your most hidden, most ashamed-of secrets. All those things that make you feel like a monster now. He will know them. And he will be proud of you. I promise.

And around that time you will stop seeing death as the only way out of all the worry and fear and anger. That desire to die will go away and in its place will be a need to be useful, and a first-time-ever comfort in being yourself. Right now you feel like an alien. I remember you telling a group of kids one night at a slumber party that you believed you were from another planet. You really believed it. And I know you do right now as you read this. You know what? You are. And it's cool. You'll find that planet years later and find other aliens and even then you'll feel different. It's how we are. You'll just get used to it and eventually even be grateful for it.

I'm closing this letter, Billy, and there's so much I want to tell you and yet I know that nothing I write or say now will change how you feel. I remember how impenetrable you were, how convinced of your aloneness. Just know that I can see you, across the years, from not so far away, I can see you clearly and I know all your worries and fears and shames and death-wishes and alien thoughts. I see and know all of it and many others will too, and they will love you, not despite those things but because of them. So just carry on, kid. Keep calm and carry on.

Love,

*Bill*

# SARAH MOON

*Dear Sarah,*

Oh, honey.

First of all, stop eating lunch in the bathroom. Go to the back stairwell to read this, no one will bother you, and there's a window. In the spring, you can eat in the parking lot. Spring'll come soon.

## ON GIRLS

You will sleep with lots of hot women. Calm down.

Later, when you're smarter, you'll sleep with *nice* hot women too.*

---

*Okay, just between you and me, we both know that the weirdest thing about coming out on your first day of high school in this tiny cow-town is that you haven't even kissed a girl yet. All you're going on is that feeling in your stomach when you see those pictures of the Spice Girls. It feels a little strange to go around proclaiming that you're a lesbian when you're not even sure that, you know, you'll like it. That quiet fear that this isn't the right thing, that you're going through all of this trouble for nothing, that if you had Angelina Jolie right there in front of you, you wouldn't know what to do with her, it's very scary. I have good news for you: The trouble is worth it, and you'll learn what to do, and that will be fun.

## ON VEGETABLES

You should eat more of them, really. Revenge on your fruit-leather-loving, cauliflower-steaming parents by refusing to eat any vegetables until you are twenty-eight is just silly. Also, as it turns out, you don't hate spinach. One day, you will have dinner parties and fill your house up with people you love and you will feed them.

And stop making fun of your father because you too will have a very particular way of loading the dishwasher.

## ON THAT BODY OF YOURS

There will be women who come up behind you and grab your hips and take your breath away. That is how you will learn to love your hips. The rest of it, though, the tiny breasts, dimpled hands, soft belly, potato-shaped feet, baby face, even that one birthmark with the terrible, occasional hair, you'll have to learn to love all of those things on your own.

## ON TOUGHNESS

You put on a leather jacket and smoke cigarettes in the parking lot. You don't tend toward classroom-appropriate language and if it weren't for a laughably lenient vice principal, you would be in a lot more trouble than you're in. All of that, sweet girl, and you're still not tough. Not in the least.

It's good news because tough is not going to do you any favors.

It's not going to make L fall in love with you, it's not going to make Christina be your friend again, it's not going to undo the spit or the names or the swastikas, it's not going to make high school go by any faster than it's going, it's not going to make you not care that your parents' divorce sucks, or make you stop thinking about Erin's death, it's not going to make Aunt Nan not have cancer, it's not going to make you feel more like your mother or your sister (who are not so tough themselves, despite what you will continue to believe for a few more years).

So relax, stop trying to perfect your scowl, take off those steel-toe boots (you know they are *not* the right size and you have blisters for weeks), quit smoking (you're asthmatic, idiot), and let yourself cry sometimes. No matter what you think, letting yourself start to cry does not mean you will never stop.

## ON FAMILY

Your whole, entire family in every single version of it that exists and will exist (this is not the last one, sadly. I know. I'm sorry.) loves you with its entire fumbling heart. I know you feel like an alien and like these people are just waiting for the day the mother ship comes to pick you up, but they're not. In fact, they each feel alien a lot of the time themselves. That's how they know that you're one of them.

Your parents and you get through this. They're pretty distracted right now; divorce does that to people. Switching houses every three days is too much for you. You want to talk strength?

Strength is being able to say, I have to stay in the same place for a little while; I can't have all of my belongings in a book bag anymore. Strength means making difficult decisions, like who to live with, and who to visit. No one's life will be destroyed by these decisions; yours, however, might be saved. And that's all either of your parents wants.

## ON HURTING YOURSELF

Please stop.

## ON THE BULLIES

How did you think you got strong?

It's terrible and scary. You are going to be fine. It is in fact true that Tim K. will pump your gas in five years, and that a slew of people will apologize and eventually some will even come out themselves. At the end of the day, you are strong and brave through this, and those are not such bad things to be.

## ON GOOD THINGS

Next semester, you will find a note in your bag. This one will not say dyke, or die, or shut up. This one will say thank you. It will be from a senior who is scared, who says you give him hope.

When you graduate, your principal (in whose office you will have spent almost your entire senior year) will give you the award for leadership; she will thank you in front of everyone for pushing her to be a better leader and for making the school a better place. It will be wrapped in a rainbow ribbon. It will not fix everything or wash away the previous years of names and thrown eggs and graffiti and fear. But it will be a good start.

You like college. You choose good friends, mostly. You become a teacher, and you are good at it, just like you'd hoped you'd be. You thank Ms. Rose for that. You write. You are not crazy. You are not mean. You are not hard-hearted and cold. In fact, your heart is big and kind and holds lots of people. You are you, just more so.


xoxoxo,


*Sarah*

# BRUCE COVILLE

*Dear Bruce-I-Used-to-Be —*

I start with that greeting because I'm who you are going to become. I hope that won't scare you too much. It shouldn't, because you're going to have a really good life. Also, for a while, a really confusing one. Which is the main reason I was so happy to have this chance to write to you. I have some important things to tell you.

First and foremost: It's going to be OK!

Second in line, and nearly as important: It's not going to feel that way sometimes, and it's definitely not going to be easy. How can it be? Most people don't even think that what you are exists.

I mean, seriously, you already know you don't quite fit in. You're just not aware, yet, how fully that is true. So, let's get it on the table: You're bisexual. Not straight. Not gay. Bisexual.

(Come on, just think about how much you like looking at the underwear ads in the Sears catalog . . . no matter which page you're on!)

The thing is, the word "bisexual" isn't easy to discover back then, especially not for a kid living out in farm country. So in a couple of years you're going to invent your own self-descriptor, just to have a name for yourself. Knowing that people who can use their right hand and their left hand with equal ease are called "ambidextrous," you will decide to think of yourself as "ambisextrous." I still think that was clever of you. (You're good with words. Stick with that: It's going to pay off.)

The good news is that your "sexual orientation," as it will come to be called, is actually pretty cool. It means there are so many more people you can have fun with. And you can take considerable pride in saying that when it comes to love you'll never discriminate on the basis of gender!

On the other hand, it's going to make life really tricky.

For one thing — and this will get really annoying — people are desperately going to want you to decide you're either straight or gay. Most will want you to be straight, because they find that more comfortable. Your gay friends, in contrast, will be rooting for you to declare yourself in their camp. Only rarely will people simply accept you for what you are. In fact, they will want "clarity" of your identity so much that they're going to tell themselves, and try to tell you, that what you are is imaginary.

I'm not kidding. Many gay folk are going to believe you just haven't finished coming out yet — or worse, that you're afraid or ashamed to admit that you're really gay. Straight folk, especially the ones who don't want you to be gay, will cling to the belief that you're "just going through a phase."

You're even going to believe it yourself for a while. When you're happily (but guiltily) exploring sex with your buddy Tom, even while you're crushing on the gorgeous-but-unavailable Cheryl, you're both going to be telling yourself that messing around with a male friend is just a substitute for "the real thing."

This will turn out to be true for Tom — and absolutely false for you.

As to the guilt . . . try to shed it as early as you can! It's an appalling artifact of a culture that is totally messed up and fearful about sexuality in all its forms. People are going to get healthier about this in the decades ahead of you, which is going to be a huge relief to everyone.

Just how tenacious is this idea that what we are doesn't exist? It still persists. Only this month I saw a report on a new study where some scientists were *amazed* to discover that there really are men who are aroused by both men and women. We could have told them that a long time ago, but they wouldn't have believed us.

To set the record (you should pardon the term) straight: By the time I'm writing this, you'll have been going through that "phase" for almost fifty years. And it shows no sign of coming to a close. (A word of advice in that regard: It pays to take care of your body. Seriously, you'll have a lot more fun if you do.)

Anyway, what you really are is Queer. Not "queer" in the sense of "a guy who only likes guys," but queer in the sense of being really, really different. You're going to find that even when you're in a subgroup you don't quite fit in.

Don't worry about it. It's a lot more interesting than being "normal" — which hardly anyone is, anyway. The whole "normal" thing is pretty much a made-up idea. And — oddly enough — even though "normal" is supposed to be the default option, and the goal, in their hearts most people want to be unique in one way or another.

On that matter, early me, we are definitely ahead of the game!

Happily, there are some real joys to come from this. A first kiss is, for most people, a once-in-a-lifetime experience. You'll have it twice, with the first girl you'll love, and later with the first man you'll love. It will be earth-shattering both times!

That's about it for now. You'll have the usual ups and downs, of course. I can think of some times that make me wish I could come back and give you a big hug and assure you it's all going to be okay. Trust me, you'll live through them, though it may not feel like it at the time. The thing is, as long as you can keep that cheerful attitude (it's one of the best things about you), you'll be fine.

You're going to love, really love, a lot of people.

And you're going to get a lot of love in return, for all kinds of things you do.

Which is pretty much the best thing that anyone can ask for.

That's it for now. Take care of yourself.

And enjoy the ride.


With love,


*Bruce-You-Will-Become*

# LaShonda Katrice Barnett

*Spring 1988*
*My dear, dear Shay,*

Y
ou've just closed the social studies text fashioned in a brown paper-bag jacket with doodled hearts and Alice's name all over it; no doubt all enthused about some pillar of United States government, since at the moment you think you will become a judge. You can't help it that you get all crazed in third period hearing about all those freedoms inherent in any worthy democracy. You've got it honest — you're an American. Of course, it doesn't help that *she* sits next to you wearing that cheerleading skirt whenever there's a home game. Not to mention, your ancestors — your skinfolk and your kinfolk (you'll learn the difference, trust me) — hoed a hard row for those liberties. For all the hoopla about freedom of speech, I wish I could tell you that you'll meet lots of people who embrace freedom of thought and freedom of loving with as much zeal. Sadly, you won't.

Still, you're off to a good start following the beat of your own zany drummer, bearing in mind that Freedom is more than a word, it's a way of life. Dear Shay, go hog wild jamming along your Freedom trail with those people who strike you for their originality, their goodness, their unabashed care and support of you, because some parts of the journey will be damn scary. I look down the road a bit to 1992 — pledge week for the sorority you dream about joining even now. The thought crosses your mind to introduce Alice (oops! Spoiler alert — yes, she feels the same way you do) as a relative instead of your lover. But it's too painful to turn something so good into something as ugly as a lie. And the people you choose along your trail will support you. Ironically, it won't be until you go to the books and cinema — they've always been your ports in a storm — that you'll get off course.

It's senior year of college and though you're president of the sorority you've gone and gotten rid of all of your pretty dresses and high-heel shoes! Feminist theory, books by Joan Nestle, Leslie Feinberg, and Lesléa Newman — not to mention films like *Go Fish* and *Bar Girls* — have you all confused. *If Alice wears dresses and makeup, can you?* Dear Shay, being queer does not mean that you have to wear flannel or steel-toe boots, unless of course you want to. You see, it's a good thing you like politics because every group has them. But, remember, you're free to be a femmy-femme girl who also loves femmy-femme girls. How else will you ever really know what other shades of lipstick look good on you? Being queer does not mean all of your books, music, and entertainment will be gay, or that your poodle-loving heart will have to adopt a cat, go vegan, and vacation in Michigan every August, although you will love the Womyn's music festival. Imagine Girl Scout camp full of adorable artsy chicks running around with their original songs, poetry, fiction, and manifestos on topics that run the gamut from what and who to eat (seitan) to which car to drive (Subaru) — in cutoff jeans and green sashes with nothing underneath. These festivals started out in the Midwest — land of your roots, Shay, so you see you've never been alone. You make it to Michigan, Indiana, Iowa, and a particularly memorable one in the woods of Pennsylvania. These girl holidaze are a Rite of Passage for you and many thousands of others.

Most important, and I know this is a big one for you, being queer does not mean that the same God everybody else calls on is somehow deaf to you. Really. Pardon me for sounding like a commercial here, but yes, you too can have a spiritual life! This will blow your mind, but like many black lesbians, you'll actually hook up with women from church — and not a "gay" church, though you will find your way to one of those too, but your traditional Baptist church. Next Sunday, open your eyes and you will see that you're already in the company of others just like you; only they are not as brave as you will need to be.

Waiting on me to tell you what your queerness means? Here's the thing, dear Shay, your queerness is going to change all of the time, like everything else about you — your skin, your hair, your distaste for tomatoes and beets, your thoughts on the literature of Baldwin and Morrison, Battle's coloratura and Parker's shrieking alto sax. What I know is this: Even in the face of all the scary shit you hear and see on the news — signs of hate ranging from the cardboard ones stapled to plywood to the tombstones bearing the names of Sakia Gunn (NJ), Jessica Mercado (CT), and Matthew Shepard (WY) — loving women does not preclude you from sharing beautiful intimacy with an amazing partner; having a child; belonging to a wonderful community; living a life of *your own design*, the life of your dreams.

Future social studies books will tell a different tale about your citizenship, one that won't have you living in a land whose twenty-first-century take on same-sex marriage is a throwback to the nineteenth-century case Plessy v. Ferguson (separate but equal). Dear, dear Shay, you must love whom you will fearlessly, remembering that as an American it is your birthright. You are free to do it.

I love you,

*LaShonda Katrice Barnett*

# HOWARD CRUSE

*Dear Howard,*

Here's a news flash from the future: Your penis is not a pervert. And neither are you.

Sure, the world has done its best to convince you otherwise with its snickers and sneers and smutty slang words ("fag"; "queer"; "cocksucker"; "fairy"). It's important to remember, though, that the "world" that's making you feel so bad is just a planetful of individual people, an astonishing number of whom are astonishingly ignorant about things they like to think they know all about.

Like homosexuality.

"Homosexuality." Now there's a word that's gotten progressively scarier whenever you've considered that it may apply to you. It's too long and cumbersome to roll off the tongues of the playground bullies, but it's the term of choice for authors, which is why you keep looking it up in book indexes.

You don't like what the book authors say about it and you don't like the word itself. Who would? It sounds like a sickness.

An undesirable "condition." You're wondering, *If I'm going to be a "homosexual," exactly how mentally ill does that make me?*

How do I know what you're wondering? I know because I *am* you — the you you're going to be half a century from now. Think time travel and you'll catch my drift. I'm weathered and creaky and my hair's thinning fast, but I still vividly remember *being* the you that you are right now. I know what's in your heart because I've been there. Literally.

So I speak with confidence gained from decades spent walking in your shoes when I say, *Forget about being "sick." You're not.* It's as simple as that.

And stop labeling yourself as "a homosexual." Sure, James Dean does a number on you the way Marilyn Monroe does a number on lots of guys your age, but that's just your individual hormones in action. And hormones are only a small part of what makes up a human being.

You're you. A person, not a sex drive. You're still the same preacher's kid who played with hand puppets and wrote radio plays and drew comic books during lazy afternoons back in Springville. You got "born again" at eight and began complaining to your dad about fundamentalism's inconsistencies by the time you were twelve. You've edited the school paper, been elected to the student government, and for a loser at athletics aren't all *that* awful at soccer. And then there's that correspondence course in cartooning you've been taking for three years. Think you might manage to sell a comic strip to some newspaper syndicate someday? You've put in plenty of hours with that dream in mind.

Those are all parts of who you are that are just as important as who gets cast in your wet dreams. Is all of that summed up by the word "homosexual"? I don't think so!

You've got to trust yourself and tune out those authors who've got so much to say about how "unnatural" homosexuality is. They're whizzes at throwing pompous psychological jargon around, but most of them know little to nothing about what makes someone like you tick.

Every year you've been getting better and better at thinking for yourself instead of automatically believing everything you read in books. So here's a perfect opportunity to practice separating wisdom from hogwash. Marshal that healthy skepticism you've been cultivating and ask: *Where's the evidence behind all that disapproval?* Does what the "experts" are selling square with what you've experienced in your own life? Does it square with common sense?

Remember the time you commented, in a paper you wrote about *Huckleberry Finn* for a literature class, that white people were inherently more intelligent than black people? Your teacher nailed you in a flash. "What's your evidence for that?" he asked.

As a kid who had grown up in rural Alabama when racial segregation ruled the South, it never occurred to you to question that assumption. The grown-ups around you, who were supposed to be the experts on how things are in life, considered the intellectual superiority of the white race to be so obvious as to need no arguments. Did anyone need evidence that the sky is blue? Hardly. Some things, you were raised to believe, are true simply because everyone *knows* that they're true.

But then your teacher's question stopped you short. You tried to think of evidence for your assertion, but nothing you came up with could stand up to scrutiny.

Those authors who are telling you how sick and morally twisted homosexuals are and how doomed they are to lives of misery got those messages from their own elders, and their assertions were no more rooted in evidence than your ideas were about the relative intelligence of blacks and whites. Since in earlier days the subject of homosexuality was considered unfit for proper conversation, attitudes about it were likely to be conveyed mainly through smirks and fag jokes, but they still got embedded in most people's psyches. And now that some of them have persuaded the editors of their books that they're qualified to compose dignified discourses on sexuality, they're passing on those attitudes to their readers.

But where is the evidence that you're sick or morally twisted? Have you noticed how their attempts to support their arguments logically can't withstand scrutiny? You need to think through these issues in light of your own real-world experiences instead of being intimidated by what you read in books.

You know that you never asked to be gay, and you weren't seduced into it either. Your attraction to other guys flowered spontaneously within you as you grew into sexual maturity. Once you do set aside what the authors, preachers, and schoolyard bullies say about it, you will know in your heart that the yearning you have to be close to other guys is natural and positive. It even feels loving, sometimes, when your crushes are on a roll.

You've got to trust your inner naturalness, Howard. It's dangerous not to. I know you've been trying as hard as you can to switch your brain into heterosexual mode, but it's not happening yet and it's never going to. That's making you feel desperate. Your black moods about what life holds in store for you have been getting darker and darker, and you've been thinking more and more about suicide as a way out. You even took a serious swing at it once. Sure, you lucked out by botching the attempt, but it's a memory that still disturbs me. It makes indulging in a little time travel today feel worth the effort.

I don't want to spoil life's interesting surprises by spilling too many beans, but given how much anxiety you have right now about what's in store for you, let me throw out a few tidbits.

That cartooning course you've been taking by mail is going to pay off, though not in exactly the way you've been envisioning. Yes, you'll get to draw a nationally published comic strip someday, but it won't be anything like *Li'l Abner* or *Peanuts*. It'll be way more satisfying.

Wanna know one reason why? Because when the time comes and you're ready to take the plunge, you're going to learn that any artist's creativity rises to new levels of power when it's rooted in honesty. Right now you're afraid that you'll never be allowed to enjoy a "real" cartooning career unless you keep readers from knowing you're gay. But here's a twist that's going to turn that fear upside down: It's when you finally feel strong enough to blow your Big Secret out of the water by letting everybody in the world know that you're gay, when you start putting your honest gay perspective into your comics with no apologies, that your talents will finally get the kind of widespread recognition you're dreaming of now. And the icing on the cake will be learning that the honesty you put into your comics will inspire new generations of kids who are struggling with *their* Big Secrets the way you've been struggling with *yours*.

Think about how scary the word "queer" has been while you've been growing up. Well, here's a switch: The time is coming when you and other gay folks like you will claim that loaded word as a badge of honor. In broad daylight, no less! The rest of the world will just have to get used to it!

Then there's sex. You can relax about that. The yearning you have to hold guys close and enjoy the sexy feelings that go with that will have its day in the sun. Yep, you're going to get plenty of chances to take those delicious desires and run with them. It's a perk of adulthood.

And what about love? Rest assured that your straight class-mates who're running off to neck at the movies every weekend won't have a monopoly on that in years to come. By the time you've become me you'll have enjoyed making a home with a terrific guy for thirty-three years. And there won't be any need to keep it a secret from the neighbors either.

I could go on and on, but filling out the full picture would take fifty years. Better that you should discover it all for yourself.

For now, just chew on the scraps of information I've been laying on you the next time those clouds of despair start descending. You still have some gloomy days to get through, like everybody else, but if you can just hang on until your dreams start getting traction, you'll be glad you did.

What a shame it would be to miss all the fun!

Your pal from up ahead,

*Howard*

# BIL WRIGHT

*Dear Bil,*

I was talking about you to a friend the other day. And before I knew it I was sitting in the same room with you at "Sister" Johnson's sweet sixteen party. We both knew Sister only invited you because she really liked your mom. It was probably your mom who told her, "You should invite Billy." So she did. You could have killed your mom. But you went. What choice did you have? Your mom said something like, "Billy, you're fourteen. This is what you should be doing. Not staying in this apartment, trying to hide out." And you got dressed knowing there was no way you were gonna look like any of the other guys there. You'd already seen a lot of them hanging out in front of Sister's building. They wore short-sleeved argyle-patterned sweaters; tight, shiny pants that made their butts look like two basketballs wrapped in colored fabric; and shoes that matched. You didn't own anything but cotton dress shirts, a navy blazer with gold buttons, the gray or navy pants you wore to church, and penny loafers. This was not gonna be fun. When you got there, all the guys and girls were already coupled up. Some were in the middle of the room dancing and the rest were sitting around the room, looking glued together, shoulder to shoulder, waiting for the lights to get turned lower so they could start making out. You could see the girls giggling as the guys' fingers inched up their skirts. As much as you thought you should, you probably wouldn't ever want to be one of those boys waiting for the lights to get turned down so you could make out with your girl. It's safe to say — is it safe to say? — what you wanted was someone's arm around you instead, so you could put your head against a strong chest and hear the music — "Ooooo — baby, baby" — and feel — there's that word again — safe.

I was telling that same friend how three years later, we were walking down Central Park West together. You don't remember I was with you, do you? It was August, at about four o'clock in the morning. You were trying to make it to 59th Street to catch the A train uptown to Harlem. You were exhausted, but you couldn't sit and rest on one of those benches that lined the park because you hurt too much. The man who lived on 96th Street and Central Park West had hurt you when you'd thought he was your friend. Sounds funny now, maybe even ridiculous. But you did. You thought maybe he was a friend and you could put your head on his chest and hear the music, just like you'd wanted to do at Sister Johnson's sweet sixteen. You thought maybe there was a chance, until you understood he wasn't your friend and it was dangerous. You asked him if you could leave, he said no, and you knew you were anywhere but safe. "I'm sorry, I have to leave now," you'd told him again, and he'd blocked his apartment door. You remembered your grandmother saying, "God gave you this body on loan. Don't mistreat it and don't let anybody else mistreat it either." But it was too late now. Now, what you wanted was to get to 59th Street to catch the A train to Harlem, where you'd feel safe.

You couldn't wait to leave home because you knew you'd never feel like one of the boys at Sister Johnson's sweet sixteen party. You'd wanted to go to New York. Your mom let you stay with your aunt for the summer, you got a job in the city, where you could buy the clothes you wanted and stay out late. Till four o'clock, if you wanted to. Sometimes, a lot of times, you'd get off the A train and the sun would be coming up and your aunt would be waiting to tell you, "Whatever you're doing isn't safe, Billy. It isn't safe." But at least nobody wanted you to go to parties to make out with a girl on the couch or to "act like a man for a change."

What I want to tell you is I saw you then, Billy, and I see you now and I wish I could have made you feel, yeah — safe. There was no way for you to know, trying to make it to 59th Street, hurting, that most people have to care about someone to want to make them feel safe. People don't often care about strangers and your life was full of strangers. You were a kid trying to make strangers your family.

Family can make you feel safe, although sometimes they don't. Friends can make you feel safe, but sometimes they don't. It's fine to look for it, lots of people do. And as I get older, I know more and more people who find it. That feeling of safety. It may not be in the form of one person. It may be a few. It may not come in the shape you thought or have the color of eyes or hair you dreamed. But it will come. Trust me on that.

I just wish, that night, I could have carried you in my arms, down along the park and up into the air over the city. I wish I could have made you feel. Safe.

Here's a hug for Billy. He was a good kid.

Love,

*Bil Wright*

# Michael DiMotta

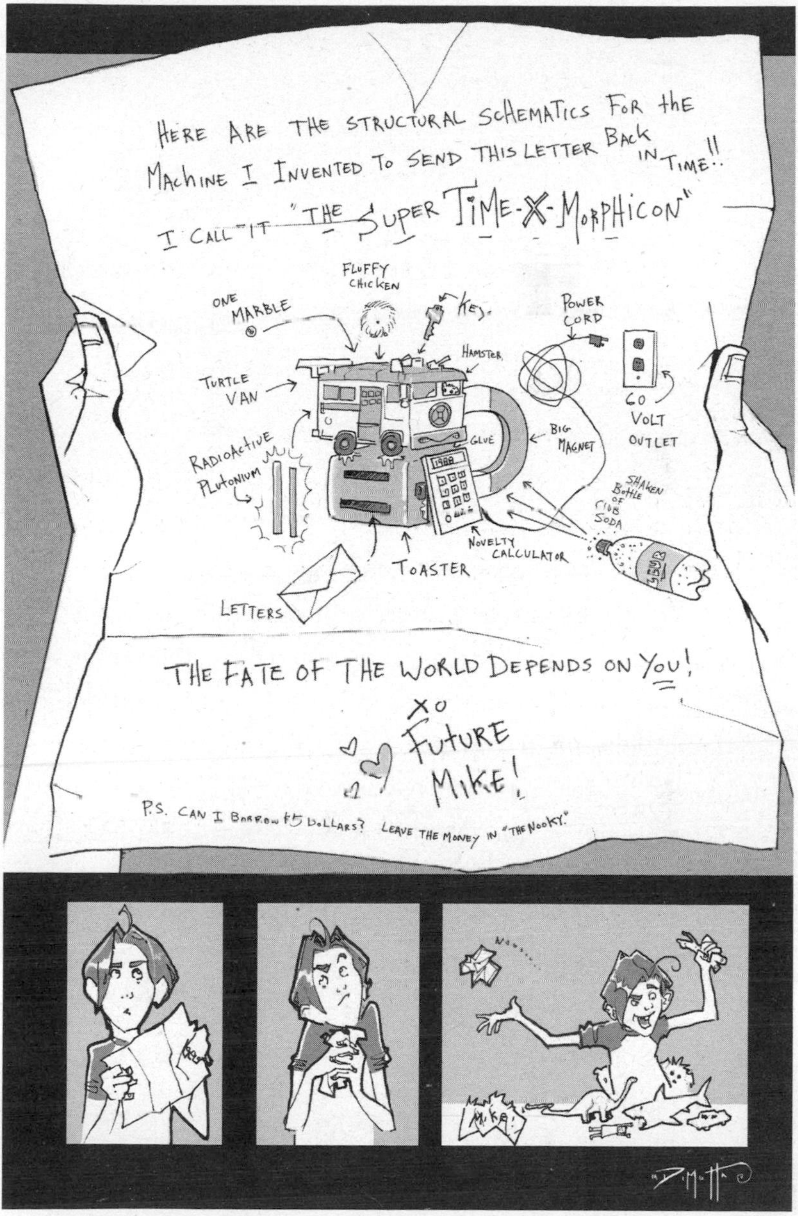
HERE ARE THE STRUCTURAL SCHEMATICS FOR THE MACHINE I INVENTED TO SEND THIS LETTER BACK IN TIME!!
I CALL IT "THE SUPER TIME-X-MORPHICON"
FLUFFY CHICKEN
ONE MARBLE
KEY
POWER CORD
HAMSTER
TURTLE VAN
60 VOLT OUTLET
GLUE
BIG MAGNET
RADIOACTIVE PLUTONIUM
SHAKEN BOTTLE OF CLUB SODA
NOVELTY CALCULATOR
TOASTER
LETTERS
THE FATE OF THE WORLD DEPENDS ON YOU!
XO FUTURE MIKE!
P.S. CAN I BORROW $5 DOLLARS? LEAVE THE MONEY IN "THE NOOKY."
MIKE!

# CARTER SICKELS

*Dear Teenage Me,*

Right now you're probably holed up in your room, reading something by S. E. Hinton or Stephen King, scribbling furtively in your journal, which, unfortunately, you'll throw away before you're twenty, embarrassed by the secret crushes, the scared questions about God and death, and the cutout pictures of Bon Jovi, Ralph Macchio, and, oh, yes, Cher during "If I Could Turn Back Time." Not to mention the bad poetry, and all your hopes and dreams about becoming a writer. Most of your peers don't know how much you love to read, that you write stories. You're so worried about what they'll think, how they'll judge you. I remember how shy you are. At school, you blend, don't draw attention to yourself. What you also don't do is protest the gay jokes or stick up for the kids who are bullied, which, if it doesn't shame you now, will later. But don't be too hard on yourself — you're scared, and right now, you don't know a single gay person. Still, I wish I could get you to join up with the boys who get called faggot, the weird kids, or the nerds who read out in the open. These are the cool ones, the fighters. They would teach you to not be ashamed. Eventually, years down the road, you'll find them, the queers, writers, artists, the trannies and drag queens, but listen, it would make your life brighter if you could start looking for them a little sooner.

The good news is that although now you're so worried about fitting in — listening to the right music, wearing the right clothes — one day, you'll stop caring so much. It won't matter anymore what the popular kids think. They're not going to be in your life after you leave this small town. You're going to make it to New York City. You'll live there for ten years, and then (I know, this part is hard to believe), you'll decide country life is more you. You're going to travel all over the U.S., you'll go to Europe. Your love for reading and writing? That's what will save you. Books already transport you, opening your mind. Keep reading, keep writing. One day, you'll meet others who love books as much as you do. One day, your dream of publishing a novel will come true.

Right now, you see things in black and white, and believe fervently in right or wrong. Heaven or hell, gay or straight, good or bad, boy or girl. But the world is not like that: nothing is permanent, and there are no definite answers, no single way of being. What if you could be handsome instead of pretty? Instead of disappearing behind shapeless shirts and baggy pants, you could dress in tight jeans and T-shirts that fall flat against your chest, just like the boys in *The Outsiders*, which you read at least a half dozen times? You'll discover that sexuality and gender do not stay still, but like clouds, shift and twist and open up in beautiful, new ways. You'll walk down paths you never thought were possible, you'll move easily in your own body, you'll answer to a different name.

You're not a freak, you're not a sinner, no matter what kids at school say, or the minister at church, or people on TV. God loves you. I wish I could tell you that things won't be difficult with your parents, but the truth is, they might not ever accept or understand you. This is not your fault, and you need to stop feeling guilty for being yourself (you'll still be working on this twenty years down the road, so try to start now). You'll have friends and lovers who support you, who love you for who you are. You need to let them in. Learn to be gentle with yourself, and forgiving — you have more strength and courage than you realize.

Sometimes I wish you were different: more gutsy and confident, maybe even more of a boy. But really I don't wish any of those things — because I know you are going to grow and change, and if you weren't the way you are now, then I would not be me. One last thing. Please don't throw away that journal. You're going to want to read it one day, trust me.


With love,


*Carter*

# DIANE DIMASSA

*Mad, Sweet Kid,*

I know why you drink. I know why you hurt yourself. I know you think you're just all wrong. You come here and I'm going to wrap my arms around you and tell you the truth. The truth is people are ugly. I know you're frightened and turned off and turned on living in Backwards Land. Everything is inaccessible and wrong in Backwards Land. All the doors are locked in Backwards Land. The town you live in is a breeding ground for generations of xenophobes, racists, and idiots. Every day in school is hell. The guys all drive jacked up vans and the girls have all had two abortions by the time they reach senior year, and you all drink Schlitz beer on the beach together. And these are your "friends"! You get drunk with them and writhe with crushes on the girls and endure "boyfriends." You see them every day and listen to them use words like "fuckin' homo" and "cunt" and worse, and you take it in and believe it because nobody is telling you any different. You keep stuffing and stifling yourself and using more drugs, and drinking the older guys under the table. You have a reputation.

You will take any mystery drug and report back, you will take any dare when you are drunk. You have been arrested, suspended, and grounded for entire summers. Finally! An identity! The white kids and the black kids in school riot often; the students stage walk-outs; the cops come and mace you all. But you like it, because it matches the chaos inside you. It is a place to explode, which you need so badly to do with nowhere to do it. Every waking moment is mental agony. Then at night, you brilliant thing, you go home and smoke a joint out the window, put your headphones on, and listen to four or five Bowie albums ("that fag"). And that is called a survival technique. And that is where you get the strength to get up and do it again. Of course you're frustrated, suffocated. And emaciated; you should eat.

You don't eat. You need to eat.

I love you. Stop hurting yourself. Listen to me.

The truth is, people are ugly and they are ignorant. They are small and wooden-headed, they are rabid and savage and full of shit and bile, and I'm telling you straight up because I will not lie to you, you need to grow a skin because the world is full of them. Those kids you go to school with will most likely grow up and turn into their parents and have kids like them. They will become the cops, the bosses, the driving instructors, the other people in the world. They're everywhere, and you have to pick through them to find your tribe. Did I mention yet that you are part of a tribe? Yes. You're outnumbered, but that is okay. Yes, there are more of you. Yes, you'll find each other. In the meantime, there is an art teacher you have. She pretends she doesn't know you are cutting class and lets you stay in the ceramics studio for hours. She says nice things to you, tells you you are talented, gently tries to point out that maybe you are hanging out with the wrong people. She may be one of your tribe; do you think? She knows that the ceramics room is a safe house for you. She sees you. She's a gift in a sea of crap. Learn to see the angels; there may be one or two more. If you don't believe in angels, call them "hope." Spots of okay-ness in a horrible minefield. Your days are hard. I want you to decide to survive it. Go out there and survive it, and eventually you'll find yourself in Slightly Less Backwards Land, or maybe even Almost Right-Side Up Land. When you get there you will be scarred, and you will be strong. Stand up straight. You are part of a family and of a chain. You are our one and only youth. You. Keep. Going. You know, someday you are going to have to reach your hand back to some little you who feels just like the you right now. Your heart will throb. Words will fail you. You have to grab the next hand. Come here, feel this. It's our heartbeat in the palm of my hand. Someone has to be there.

I love you. I am here.

I know. You don't trust anyone but yourself. Monsters arrived arm-in-arm with your adolescence. A rush of hormones and chemicals that was too much to handle. Hormones that were new, and chemicals that weren't right. It wasn't your fault. Your little brain wasn't right (it was a "mood disorder," my love) and then the drugs and the drinking and the mental torture and what a mess, trying to stay upright with the weight of all the planets on your skinny little back.

It all started so young and now you're pretty messed up, self-hammered into impossible shapes for so long. And my God, you still got up every day and endured your life. You've pulled together a little stick nest the best you could, and I give you a lot of credit for that. What I'm trying to make you know is that it changes. This moment right now . . . you're not stuck in amber; your reality, it's gonna change. You'll finish school, you'll get jobs, you'll move, you'll meet new people. Everything changes. If there is one thing I want you to remember it is that everything passes. When you feel you just cannot stand whatever it is for one more minute, remind yourself that it is temporary. I didn't say the world is going to change much. It does and it doesn't. It's not easy for anyone, and honey, it's even harder for you. I know it doesn't feel like it, but every time you go through something difficult, you get stronger. Look how much you have already survived. You are coping! I know at your age everything feels like forever. But the gears will mesh, you'll get some traction, and you'll go. You will! There is so much waiting there.

You are awaited. So keep going!

What can I say when I know you can't hardly hear me through the self-hatred and the high and you are too busy drawing nooses on your notebook? You are so wasted. Look at me. I love you for exactly all the reasons everybody else wants to burn you at the stake.

I love you *because* of the clothes. I love you *because* of what you Want. I love the broken mold you kicked away. I love you because you have Godzilla inside you. Read that again. Stick it on your chest. Tape it to your soul. Chew it up slowly, close your eyes, and swallow it.

And don't you let anybody steal or stomp it out of you. You come here and I'm going to tell you a truth. The truth is, there is nothing wrong with you. There was never anything wrong with you.

I love you. Be here.

*Diane*

# BRENT HARTINGER

*Hey Teenage Me:*

First things first: Take out a huge loan right now and invest it all in two companies: Microsoft and Starbucks Coffee. After you become a multibillionaire, set a billion or so aside and invest it all the first time you hear of a company with the weird-sounding name of "Google." Trust me on this.

Okay, now on to the *important* stuff.

Everyone always says there are three important "legs" under life: love, career, and family. I'd add a fourth: friends.

If you manage to get three out of these four things right, you'll be way ahead of most people. And as chance would have it, you have a shot at all four. Which is great because then you have enough legs to support a whole dining room table, and *that* means you don't have to eat on the floor.

Let's start with love, because that's the most fun. You're going to end up with a really great guy — a *phenomenally* great guy. A guy who, when your friends complain about how rotten their boyfriends and girlfriends are, you'll nod sympathetically, but secretly think to yourself, "Wow, I can't relate."

But the thing is, you won't end up with him by playing it safe.

That's partly Jay's fault. Spoiler alert! Jay is the guy before the guy you end up with, and he'll break your heart. Oh, God, will he break your heart! Just absolutely stomp on it, and then when he's done stomping, he'll take the Ginsu knives and just slice it all to smithereens.

And here's the thing: After getting your heart broken by Jay, you'll be really wary of getting into another relationship and of love in general. You'll think, "Screw this! All this pain isn't worth it!"

Yes, it is. First, keep in mind that, before the breakup, you and Jay will have a pretty great time, if you know what I mean. And you don't want to miss Jay in a Speedo, trust me.

So there's that.

But second, remember that love doesn't always end like it does with Jay

A lot of people think that being droll and bitter and cynical is somehow hip and edgy and cool, and maybe it is. But it's also cowardly — and more than a little lonely. People act that way because they're afraid of getting hurt.

Don't be that guy. Be cautious with sex, but open to love. Weirdly, a lot of people get that exactly backward. But it's one of life's strange paradoxes that the only way to find true love is to be willing to risk being devastated by losing it.

Who knew love was so much like a *Star Trek* episode?

So . . . about your career.

The truth is we'll make a lot of really, *really* stupid mistakes in our career. That play production in Los Angeles? What a fiasco! And you'll listen to a *lot* of Hollywood producers spew a *lot* of Hollywood bullshit.

But there's an old saying that you learn a lot more from failure than you do from success (although in success's defense, it's still a lot more fun!). What does it mean when a professional associate — an editor or an agent — supports you when you're on the top of the world? That that editor or agent is not an idiot. It's when things start to flag and someone still supports you — *that's* how you know they're the real deal. That's how you know they believe in *you*.

Anyway, trust me on this: Just roll with all of it. Remember what I said about how important it is in love to be willing to take chances? That's true in your career too. In other words, not only does this essay have a recurring theme, so does your life.

At one point, someone will say to you, "Would you be willing to teach in a college?" You'll think they're crazy — and you'll be terrified that you'll fall flat on your face. But if you're willing to take a chance, it turns out you'll be pretty good at it. And you'll have a blast.

The weird thing is you'll be pretty good at a lot of things you never even considered. But the only way you'll ever learn that is by being willing to risk looking like a complete idiot.

Which, um, you definitely will sometimes. I don't want to sugar-coat things, so I should point out that as much as you might like to be, you're never going to be an actor. Now, I'm not telling you not to audition for that play in college, just . . . write your lines from the top of the second act on your hand, okay? That's all I'm sayin'.

Does failure suck? Does it hurt? Oh, it so does. But it doesn't kill you. And as a philosopher you haven't studied yet once said, whatever doesn't kill you makes you stronger.

Seriously, it's the people who never look like idiots who should be embarrassed, because that means they never took any risks. How pathetic is that?

What about your friends?

Here's one thing you and I have a pretty good instinct for, and you'll almost always get right: your friends. You'll meet plenty of mean, arrogant, ignorant, bitchy, and/or full-of-it people. You can definitely ignore *them*. Just keep searching for the smart, thoughtful, considerate, kind, interesting ones. Sadly, it's not always obvious which is which at first, so here's the test: Just as with professional colleagues, it's the ones who believe in you, the ones who stick around when times are bad. This is another reason why failure is so important: It shows you — loudly and clearly — exactly who your real friends are.

Oh, and the really great people? They don't always look and act like you do, and aren't necessarily even the same approximate age or race or weight as you. So completely disregard all that stuff.

Once you find your core circle of good friends — and there are only maybe ten truly fantastic ones in all — man, hold on to them for dear life. Be just as supportive and loyal to them as they are to you. And if ever in life, you start to think, "Oh, my God, I'm such a loser!" just open your eyes and look around you at all these terrific folks who love you.

You think these great people would hang around a loser? Not a chance.

We're stupid, you and I, but it turns out we have a pretty good heart. Who knew?

Finally, we come to the last leg on the clunky metaphor of life's dinner table: family. I could go into detail here, but I think you get the point: Stay open, take chances, risk failure, lather, rinse, repeat.

For what it's worth, I know it seems scary, this life of ours. Truthfully? Sometimes you should be scared. Life can get pretty shitty — more than you know right now, actually.

But hey, it can also be pretty wonderful — also more than you know right now. And when all is said and done, the wonderful parts really do outweigh the shitty parts. And even the shitty parts, well, like I said, they're there for a reason.

That's all I have for now, but you and I really should get together sometime. Call me — we'll do lunch! Do you love sushi yet? If not, I'll introduce you to it and blow both our minds.

*Brent Hartinger*

P.S. No, I'm not going to tell you the name of the great guy you end up with! Would you really want to know? Come on — we both know we're not the kind of person who reads the last chapter of a book first. But I *can* tell you he looks pretty smokin' in a Speedo too.

# Mayra Lazara Dole

Mayrita,

I hear you say, *I want to die,* and it tears at my soul that you're only thirteen and ready to give up on life.

I wish you could have told me — your older self — what was happening and I'd have jumped to help:

*A girl jammed a gun to my head and pulled my hair so hard my knees buckled. She hissed, "Disgusting tortillera. If you don't change, I'll kill you!" I knelt before her, begging, "Please don't kill me. I'll do anything you want."*

That's criminal! I'd have told you. It twists my heart to see you collapsed on your bed, writhing in pain, sobbing and trembling with fear. Hurry! Tell someone you trust so they find help.

*I can't. Three months ago I was kicked out of school for a love letter my girlfriend wrote me about our first time. It was snatched from my hand and read aloud by my teacher. It was so humiliating.*

*My best friend since first grade isn't allowed to see me. Friends won't let me sign their yearbooks. Bullies keep hounding me with, "Fags and dykes should be shot to death!" Everybody hates me. No one talks to me anymore.*

Stop haters from tormenting and terrifying you. Call the cops, or it'll take years of anguish, suffering, and struggles before you finally run.

*The girl told me if I call the police she'll blow my brains out. Bullies have some of my friends and neighbors behind them, cheering them on. Everyone thinks I deserve it. No one cares if I live or die. I can't take it anymore. I know what to do for this pain to stop.*

You're going to kill yourself for idiots?

*There's no hope. Can't you see? I'm cornered. I'm trapped. It's not worth living so alone and hated by everybody. It's too painful.*

Shhh . . . I'm wrapping you now in your old baby blanket to see if it eases your pain.

It's good that you're crying. Go ahead. Let all the pain out. I'll hold you in my arms and sing Mami's sweet lullaby; it'll soothe you. *Duérmete mi niña, duérmete mi amor, duérmete pedazo de mi corazón. Sleep my little girl, sleep my little love, sleep little piece of my heart.*

*That makes me miss the time Mami loved me. She keeps getting anonymous letters from neighbors saying, "Leave our barrio! We don't want lesbians or fags corrupting our children."*

*Now we've got to move. Mami says it's all my fault. I've ruined everyone's life. I don't want to live anymore. I've got to end it.*

No! If you won't get help or call the authorities, run away! Here's money for a Greyhound bus ticket and the name of a civil rights attorney to look up in San Francisco. Get away from here. They'll accept you with open arms and keep you safe.

*I have no money and nowhere to stay. I'll be homeless. Cops will drag me back. Mami will be even more upset. People are the same everywhere.*

That's not true. There are many gay kids, teachers, and nuns in your school who'll secretly embrace you. Your fifth-period Spanish teacher, the one who wears a tight bun at the back of her head and laughs at your classroom antics, will understand.

J, the secretary forced to translate to your mom the letter your girlfriend wrote you, is a lesbo!

Mari C, the plump girl who sits at the back of the class with long bangs covering her pale, somber face? One day, you'll meet her at a lesbian bar in Miami dancing with Anna, Lori, and C. She'll be happy, laughing and talking, and so will you.

C — the witty, curly-haired, blonde tenth grader always tossing political jokes around — and you will be close friends for a while (if you know what I mean!). She's now a lesbian attorney!

You could talk to any one of them. They're just like you and won't push you away.

And get this: The girl with the gun ended up having a drag-queen younger brother. Candela prances around wearing Spandex minidresses, glittering eyelids, screaming lipstick, and scandalous, ten-inch heels.

Stand up to those wretched nuns who won't allow you back to school next year. Tell them what they're doing is against the law. Many are frustrated lesbians. They only dream about loving the way you and your girlfriend do.

*You're lying to make me feel better. But it isn't working. I feel like throwing up. I know what to do to make the pain stop for good. Maybe then they'll all be sorry.*

No! Don't get back at everyone by dying. Get back at them by living and saving lives, starting with your own. Fight for your life! You're wasting your precious time being plagued by fear. Don't give tyrants the pleasure of seeing you lifeless in a coffin. The pain will end when you fight back! Start a Gay and Straight Alliance that raises awareness and shouts, LOVE not H8!

*Are you nuts? I'm scared to walk down the street, much less stand up for my rights! You're so naïve, for being older than me. It's too late. There's nothing to live for.*

It's people like you who've survived bullying by standing up for their rights that have ended up changing laws. You kill yourself, and bullies win again. Then they'll just terrorize more LGBTs.

This will be hard to believe, but Mami will one day accept you. She comes to love and understand you, no matter what.

You'll have true, fun friends.

You'll meet the love of your life who adores you (and you her!).

You'll write books, and have thousands of LGBT and straight fans who'll love and respect you! They'll write you emails saying, "You've changed my life!"

Many who experienced the same horrors you're going through now wanted to kill themselves too, until they read your first novel. They learned their lives could have meaning if they find support. You will literally save lives!

*I will?*

Yes! Take action and a whole new world will open up to you.

Life is a mystery where fantastic things can happen from one minute to the next, but only if you stay alive and fight for your life!

So go now — run!

# BENOIT DENIZET-LEWIS

*Dear Benoit,*

You're gay. Hooray!

Your best friend, Daniel, isn't. Unfortunately. The good news is that, before you know it, you will meet boys like Daniel who are gay. And they will love you the way Daniel cannot. And they will tell you so and show you so.

If there is a God, he loves you too. If God is a lesbian, she loves you.

Speaking of lesbians, I know you have a crush on the lesbian at the coffee shop who looks like a boy. Get used to it. When you're older, you will have a crush on a famous lesbian television star named Ellen DeGeneres, and you will live in a neighborhood with lots of lesbians, and some days you will wonder — or your friends will wonder for you — if you were meant to be a lesbian.

You will have lots of friends.

Try being vulnerable in front of them — they'll like you for it. You don't have to pretend like you can't be hurt. Everyone can be hurt. It's okay to be hurt, to show hurt.

It's also okay to be scared, to not know what to say or what to do when you're sitting at the corner of Castro and Market waiting for the bus home from school. It's 1989, and you're fourteen, and gay people are dying of AIDS, and you don't know what the hell is going on or if you will grow up to be like them, smoking and laughing and dancing and dying. But try not to judge them. They are brave. They are beautiful. They are scared. You are all those things too.

Some of your teachers are gay. You can tell them the truth.

You are a gay jock. You don't know this now, but this will bring you currency in a few years.

Speaking of sports, when you're older you will join a gay basketball league, a gay tennis league, a gay softball league, and a gay flag football league. Who knew?

Your mom doesn't know much of anything about you. She thinks she does, but she's too depressed, too judgmental, to know you. She is scary. When you're older she will learn to love you the way a mother should, but right now she is incapable of it. It has nothing to do with you. You are the most lovable boy in the world.

Your dad loves you, but he doesn't always say the right things. When you come out to him during college, for example, he will say to you, "Well, I guess this is what I get for raising you in San Francisco." Your dad will say this because he's scared. A few years after that, though, he won't be scared anymore, and he will invite you and your boyfriend over for dinner. And it will be the most normal dinner in the world.

Keep a journal.

Learn to cook.

Buy stock in a company called Apple.

I know that there isn't much to watch on television right now that can be described as "gay affirming," but when you're older there will be an entire channel, Logo, devoted to gay programming. You won't end up watching a reality show titled *The A-List: New York*, because cattiness will never appeal to you.

You know the porn videos you found in your dad's dresser when you were eleven? I'm sorry you found them. You were just a kid.

You don't have to have sex with people who don't love you, who don't know you.

You don't have to pretend to be anything you're not. You don't have to "act gay," or "act straight." You don't have to "act" at all.

You have many talents, but fashion is not one of them.

Your talents, to name a few: Being a good judge of character. Not causing harm. Throwing a football. Parallel parking (but don't try that yet). Ping-Pong. Singing in the shower.

Always remember: The more homophobic someone is, the more likely it is that they hate themselves. Their words and hate mean nothing except that they are in pain.

You are worthy of love.

You are worthy of respect.

It's okay that your friends make fun of you for liking folk music. It will make a comeback!

In a nutshell . . . I love you. Go forth, my younger self, and be happy!

*Benoit*

P.S. Isn't it weird receiving a letter from your older, wiser self? You're probably wondering a few things, like, what the hell does this older, supposedly wiser version of me look like? Well, though I am thirty-six, I'm told that I don't look a day over twenty-eight. So, while you didn't get the fashion gene, you did get the youth gene. Hooray!

# SUSAN STINSON

*Dear youth,*

I am fifty. I know you, but maybe not as well as I think I do. We've got the same hair; I still do the long, snarly thing, although I spent some decades as a short-haired bearded lady. Can you imagine? I'm pretty sure you can't. Also, the tips are brown and the roots are gray. So you made it. This far at least.

Hon, what can I tell you? (Not that you're asking me.) I remember how you used to go after wisdom in the '80s once you got to college. You'd go to lectures and readings by almost anyone, really, as long as they had put up a flyer. More than once, you were the only person attending who didn't know the speaker. You'd sit there listening to Robert Creeley (his poetry made you feel like you were levitating) or Judy Chicago (arguing in your head, impressed), trying to get the skills and attitude you needed to become the kind of writer who was an artist. You figured you'd have to sacrifice, everybody said so, but looking for what to sacrifice didn't seem like the right way to go about it.

But this is getting all *Star Trek* wormhole time warpy (don't be embarrassed; there turns out to be such a thing as nerd chic), since I'm wanting to talk to you before all that, in high school, when you are struggling more than you know how to admit. You already have friends you tell everything to, or almost everything, but, oh, darlin', the confusions of intimacy, uncertainty, and desire get you pretty deep into some messes. That warm, excited feeling when your best friend French-braids your hair or tenderly touches your face to correct your makeup deficiencies? You're both feeling it and it scares her even more than it scares you. That's why it ends so abruptly.

Oh, and the yearning. You want experience: touch, sex, tenderness, enlightened public appreciation. You want to be dancing between your friends as they do their elaborate steps and twirls, part of the connection, central to the rhythm, not huddled at a tiny table, waiting. You want to kiss her cherry-cola lip-glossed lips, again, more, longer, in a way that counts. You want to be able to talk about all of it until you figure it out. You want to write something incredible, a book. You want to see New York City, where you think glory lives. You already have a romance with the light brown color of Colorado dirt and the way grasses in the park go gold and dry in the summer to whisper above you when you stretch out on your back to watch the sky. You're right: That's hot.

It's brutally clear how low you fall on the high school scale of beauty. You're fat, off the scale of hotness altogether. I say this tenderly, with matter-of-fact affection; being fat is a fact about you that doesn't need a euphemism any more than being queer does.

There's a group now called NOLOSE: http://www.nolose.org/. Check it out and get back to me after you've played water volleyball in a Lurex cocktail dress.

Actually, you're exquisite. You really are. You've got everything you need to do the things you're dreaming of in this world. Your parents are rock solid, full of what Saul Bellow (you'll be a little shocked by how much you enjoy his work) called "potato love." It's the ordinary, daily stuff that shapes everything. They'll do their best with whatever you throw their way, and their best is exactly the kind of wisdom you're reaching for, right there for you with the banana and Grape-Nuts every morning.

I've spent the past few years asking friends who are martial artists and dancers to teach me how to fall. I'm still not that good at it, but I've rolled down a grassy hill with an egg tucked into my bra, and nothing broke. The key seems to be not to worry too much about which way is up. Just roll.

I love you. I trust you. Read a lot. When in doubt, go for empathy. Talk and work. Try to do something. You'll be fine.


Thrive,


*Susan*

# Marc Wolf

*Hey there, Marc.*

I'm looking at this picture of you at camp. How old are you? Nine? Ten? Such a great picture of a great dork. I love it! You look so awkward, and yet, so ready for fun. Posing, yet somehow relaxed. In your favorite clothes. A huge T-shirt, whose colors can only be described as Sears Roebuck hideous — primary blue sleeves, two-inch bands of white wrapping around the arm at the shoulder, Robert Indiana green for the body, finished with a half-inch blue band at the collar. I remember that shirt so well. One of my two favorites. And the pants: peppermint pink, striped with white and red. White Keds sneakers with a simple red line to match the pants.

For this picture, posing in the green doorway of a brown cabin at sleepaway camp, your arm placed so strangely along the frame of the door, it's obvious you have chosen your favorite outfit.

And now thirty-eight years later, seeing you there, I love that you mismatch so profoundly and yet wear it so proudly. It is hideous, and you seem so happy in it. That's what I want you to retain. Joy of living in what you love, despite the fact that things never seem to match. Joy of living with what you love, despite the fact that things never seem to add up.

You have yet to be almost killed on your bicycle by a drunk driver, yet to be nearly gunned down by Yugoslavian soldiers on the Albanian border, you have yet to fall in love, you probably have yet to kiss a girl. Let alone a boy. You have yet to have your heart broken, yet to tell Mom and Dad you are gay, yet to experience traveling alone around the world.

You look ready for the adventure. But you look so shy too. And that will be your battle in life, so get ready. Your love of adventure and exploring the world and the people in it, but your exhaustion from being out in that world. An exhaustion that I think just comes from your fear of not adding up.

I think anything I tell you that's worth telling, any advice I have, I still have to tell myself every day. Be brave. Be brave. Be brave. Strangely, it seems for you and me that being brave is almost harder to do with friends than it is with enemies. So yes, be brave as you fight for justice and against those who perpetuate cruelty. But please remember to be brave in your generosity, be brave in helping those close to you. Be emotionally brave to share your feelings, your thoughts. Be brave in sharing your encouragement, sharing your time. These are "soft" braveries, but they will be important for both of us. This kind of bravery exposes us because we reveal what moves us, we reveal who we really care about. And so we risk being ridiculed, especially from Dad. We risk people taking advantage of our kindness. You will even have nightmares of being laughed at by Dad and by the whole world. But by being brave in these ways now, you will help this old man writing to you learn who he is. You will help both of us become ourselves in the big world.

And when all else fails, when you're feeling like everyone is against you, help those less fortunate than yourself. Do it. Even if it's a baby bird. This is going to sound ridiculous and embarrassing to bring up, but I bring it up as a favor to ask of you more than as advice to give. Remember when Mom totally flipped out because you were supposed to be watching Ralph, but you forgot about him because you were setting up your toy farm animals, and Ralph wandered out of the house. And instead of listening to her scream at you again, you ran out and over to Peter's house, and he had borrowed your favorite record of the story of *Big Red*, and he broke it and you got in a fight and he punched you in the stomach and you ran away from him too. And then walking home through the woods, you just sat down and cried because it seemed no one was understanding you, or even liking you. And you heard that baby bird peeping and peeping, and you found it on the ground all alone. You brought it home and miraculously this one lived! And just by caring for it, all those other problems lifted.

And also remember that on the days you volunteer to read to the younger kids who are having trouble at school, it makes you realize how truly lucky you are to be able to give to others. Doing these things is good practice. Keep expanding on it. I'm serious: Save baby birds. Help those less fortunate. In the end, it's how you'll save us both.

I love you,

*Marc*

# LUCY KNISLEY

# NICK BURD

*Dear Nick,*

Yあ're not bisexual. There will be a purple night by a country club pool where you will tell your father this is what you are, but it isn't true. It's a lie that will dangle from your mouth like a hook from the lip of an almost-caught fish, inflicting pain-by-proxy on all those you present it to. It will remain until one night in college when the beautiful and extremely willing Sarah C. shows up drunk on your porch in a very small dress and you find yourself saying, "I can't." And just like that, the hook will detach. You will become the redeemed trout, the happiest one in the lake.

A piece of advice: When a boy you love has swum out into the ocean and is waving at you from an undulating spot beyond the breakers, swim out to him. Don't hesitate or second-guess. Just go. There are no sharks in the world. No one has ever drowned. The bottom might slide away from your feet, but it is still there. And this has nothing to do with your height, which isn't as bad as you sometimes make it out to be. When it comes to the depths of the ocean, height is irrelevant. Even giants experience the feeling of the bottom sloping out from under them.

There are things you cannot change, so make do.

Things you can change: your hesitancy, your death fear, your ambivalence about all the things at the bottom of the ocean that might devour you toes-first. Focus on the fact that those really are diamonds on the surface of the water, that the element of surprise can allow you to overtake the horizon. Remember, you can hold your breath forever. When the waves roll in to push you back, go under and swim below them. Do you feel that subtle rush along your back? That's you slipping out of time. When you come back up, congratulations: You are in the future.

Your heart will get wonderfully broken by a motley crew of sighing actors, trust fund drug addicts, junior therapists, freelance bartenders, orally fixated ravers, and perversely undergarmented young professionals. I won't tell you too much about these people, as that would ruin most of the fun. I will say you have my — and the entire world's — permission to cry over them all you want. But take care not to drown in your tears. There is an elusive border dividing the great nation of Self-Respect from the third world country called Wallowing. Try your best not to cross into it, as it's an embarrassing stamp to have on your passport.

You will play a role in the heartbreak of a focus group consisting of orally fixated actors, junior drug addicts, trust fund therapists, perversely undergarmented bartenders, freelance ravers, and sighing young professionals. You will love some of them, and it will be very good. Then one day you won't or he won't, or you'll both realize it wasn't love at all. Some will disappear completely from the channel of your life. Others will appear in friendly syndication. Some will appear on corners on Tuesday afternoons while you are checking to see if you have enough cash for both an iced coffee and a chocolate croissant. This will sometimes happen hundreds of miles from the place you both met and left them, and you will realize the past is chasing you with a knife in its teeth and a daisy in its hand. Smile at these people even if you don't want to. Men are handsome when they smile.

Leave home. Fail marvelously, and succeed even better. Kick your feet up and wonder when you will be back. Stay out late. Make telephone calls from unfamiliar street corners. When your mother's voice comes from far away and asks where you are, squint down the road and tell her you aren't sure. Make uncertainty your home. Put the mat out for yourself. Look at your watch and think of how you're almost home.

Go to bars alone, or maybe with a book. Glance at strangers from across the cedar-walled room. If they smile, go to them. If they lip-synch along to whatever song is playing, pretend you never saw them. Go to dinner alone, or maybe with a book. When the waiter comes, play a game where you try to get him to sit across from you without actually asking him to do so. After two desserts, stumble into the night with the wrong copy of your receipt. Leave the green stocking cap you love in the back of a cab and spend the evening convincing yourself that it doesn't matter. Throw an impromptu funeral. Invite all your clothes.

Don't take yourself too seriously. It's very cool to be gay, and being gay is very cool. When you realize that someone doesn't like you, don't dwell on it. You do not need everyone to like you. Anyone who feels they need to be liked by everyone most likely doesn't realize how exhausting this would be if it were to actually happen. Be thankful that there are those who want to ignore you. There is only one you. Charge admission.

Don't be judgmental. It pulls you out of your body and leaves you outside the party.

Take care of your body. You will be stuck in it for all your life, so treat it well. There will be days or seasons where you find yourself less than pleased with it, but this is natural. Outrun these moments. Quitting cigarettes will be a pain in the ass, so never start. Floss. Drink lots of water. Put on a good pair of shoes and go for as far as you can. When you look in the mirror, smile and say hello.

A general rule: The truth is always obvious. If something feels wrong, it is probably wrong. Do not rehearse rageful soliloquies on sleepless nights or practice insults to toss like grenades at those who have insulted you before. Be forgetful. Breathe good air and stretch out on the grass. Squint at the sky and listen to birds. If something feels right, it is probably right.

Don't worry so much. Let it all go. And if there's ever an emergency, you can always write it down.

Love,

*Yourself*

# RAY DANIELS

*Dear Ray,*

Do you remember Thrift Town?

No, not the Goodwill — that one was walking distance from the house (and you were over everything within walking distance from home) — and not the Salvation Army either — everyone and their dog went there (you wouldn't go near that one). Thrift Town was the best: way past the high school, past the mall, all the way down Park Row until it intersected with Center. Left on Center, twenty-six red lights past that (you counted, I remember), and almost there when Indo-European Foods popped up, next to the row of Vietnamese restaurants that your part of town had never even heard of.

You went there (so you said) for the Levi's and the flannels. Who cared if they fit, the baggier the better, and so what if the sleeves on the shirts were too long. You thought, "Roll 'em up, whatever" (you still think it; the sleeves will always be too long).

You weren't there for those things, though, not really. You knew then as well as you still remember that now. You just needed to bring home evidence to prove where you'd been all day, so your grandparents would believe you when you swore you hadn't been at your boyfriend's.

And though you lingered at the suits for a little while longer than the jeans, maybe you touched the lapels and slipped on a few jackets, they mostly reminded you of the elephant men who must have dined (and dined and dined) in them, then died. And that just made you feel sad. And small-boned. So mostly you rushed by those too.

I know what you really went for. How you opened the door and the fan greeted you and blew hot air into your face, then clicked and looked the other way as you rushed down the aisle to the back. Past all the clothes and shoes and toys and couches and books eyeing you. You went as far back as you could go, to the last row of the last shelf in the back room, where nobody went, to the junk boxes where nothing inside made sense. They made sense to you, and you pulled out all the treasures you'd keep for the afternoon: a blue umbrella, a white china teacup, somebody's family photos, a green suitcase, a straw hat.

You lined them up on the Thrift Town floor, and for a brief moment, you could see a rainy day on a city street, your reflection in the window of a café where two women sipped tea from white china teacups. You could see yourself, standing beneath your blue umbrella in a fine suit and a felt fedora, with a suitcase full of somebody's family photos in your hand. You could see yourself, on your way to somewhere else, bigger than the holes you kicked in the walls at home, more beautiful than the sound of the slamming front door, more curious than the girl with the bowling shoes and the nights of question marks in her room. You could see it all, in a flash, on the Thrift Town floor. Some bigger place, some better time.

And you were right.

Love always,

*Ray*

# JAMES LECESNE

*Dear Jimmy,*

So the first thing you should know is that I changed our name. I'm called James now. When I moved to New York City to fulfill your dream of becoming an actor, writer, and international bon vivant, James just seemed to better express the person we hoped to become. I'm not sure that I've lived up to the *international bon vivant* part, but I have traveled some, and as it turned out, being an international bon vivant was not as exciting (or profitable) a pastime as it may have seemed when you were thirteen and living in a New Jersey suburb. Also, by the late twentieth century, opportunities for bons vivants had all but died out, and I discovered that there were so many other and greater things to be in this world. I did keep our last name. Even though Lecesne has proved very difficult for strangers to spell and to pronounce, it is distinctive, memorable, and much later when you are in middle age, you will discover things about your ancestors that will blow your mind and make you proud to bear the name.

But I'm not here to ruin the surprise by telling you how your life turns out. I wouldn't dream of taking away the fun or spoiling the challenges that come with living a full-throttle Life devoted to Art and Love and Spiritual Truth. I just want to encourage you to trust yourself as much as you can, as often as you can. You do, in fact, know the score and though you may not know how to sing it loud and proud, you can hum the tune just fine — even now.

For instance, the fact that you've taken to hanging out in the Art room of your all-boys high school shows that you've got some sense. You possess an inner compass, something that will always tell you what's up, where to go, and who to avoid. Trust that. The Art room is so much safer than those long hallways where you often have to fend off a random shove or suffer a coarse remark. Also, the Art teacher, Mr. Livorgna, sees you and knows that you're a complicated kid with a good heart; he recognizes that something is urging you on and refusing to cave even when it would be much easier to be like everybody else. Your swish, your lisp, your insistence that people be kind, and your over-the-top enthusiasm, these are expressions of the real you, and they slip out when you aren't paying attention, when you forget to put forward that toughened and fabricated self. Unlike the other teachers, Mr. L. doesn't have a problem with the Real You or the way you are naturally; you can let your guard down, and you are smart to gravitate toward people like him, people who seem to genuinely like you. There will be many such people in your life. Look for them and stick with them.

Of course you'll occasionally get mixed up with people you don't like; you might even have to hang out with people who seem to hate you. This is just what happens. Trust that too. If you're smart and you pay attention, you'll learn the most from people who are different from you. For example, not everyone shares your aspiration to love the world. Not everyone made a vow at seven years old to love everyone without exception. And hardly anyone lies in bed at the end of the day like you do, obsessively reviewing the day, trying to determine who, if anyone, has been left outside the circle of love. Some people, like your sixth-grade teacher, Sister Maura, might understand this impulse to love everybody, but just like you she has difficulty making it happen 100 percent of the time. Remember when she called you out in front of the classroom and accused you of being a daydreaming sissy? You weren't able to stand up to her at the time, but here is what I'm suggesting — if you should see her again, explain to her that you were dreaming of the day when your idea catches on and when even she, a Catholic nun, can love and cherish every one of her students — even the gay ones. When you encounter people who have small minds or tiny hearts (like Sister Maura), try not to be too discouraged. Don't take it personally and don't waste time convincing yourself that they have the right idea. They don't. Remind yourself that they may be members of your species, but they do not belong to your tribe — and you won't belong to theirs. Go find your own people. And don't allow anyone to make you feel bad because of who you are. Ever.

You're not going to believe me when I tell you this, but the very things in your life that seem to be depressing and oppressing you right now are going to be the means by which you set yourself free. The experience of being invisible to the people you love and the suspicion that you have to keep your true self a secret from them, these things will pass as you come to know yourself better. And all the crap that is causing you to want to harm yourself will become the basis for the Art you make. Because you know what it's like to not be accepted for who you are, because you suffered and survived the bullying, you will be able to help others who are on the outside wanting in. You will be able to make them laugh and cry (sometimes both at the same time), and because you've been there and back, you'll be able to express the full spectrum of human emotions. In the meantime, learn to value what is difficult and painful without reveling in it too much. I don't necessarily believe that everything happens for a reason, but I do hold to the notion that we must find a good reason for everything that happens. So if you don't make it into that fancy college or if you miss an opportunity that you believe was meant for you (like starring in the touring company of *A Chorus Line*), don't despair. Trust that your life is happening exactly as it should so that you can become the person you always wanted to be.

Okay, now for the Love part. This is big. And I'm going to tell you straight out — You WILL find Love. It will take some time, but you will fall truly, madly, deeply, and finally in love. But keep in mind that though there will be many false starts, every one of them will be true — both men and women will do their best, as will you, to bring out the best in one another. Each great love will lead you to a deeper understanding of what Love can and cannot do. For example, if you hadn't fallen in love that first time with

John, you wouldn't have known what to do when you fell in love with Polly the following summer, and it was Polly who taught you that you might be better off with boys, and on and on. Every love has its lesson, and getting it right may take some time, but this is because while your peers are busy impressing themselves on top of girls in the backseats of cars, renting tuxedoes and coming into their own, you will be trying desperately to pass. In a world where emotional development depends on a person's ability to participate, you will fall behind a bit. You'll take to your room, imagine that you understand the lyrics of popular singing divas, sulk, decoupage your lunch box, make hand puppets with human hair, opt for style, read Jane Austen, get cast in a musical. Enjoy all that, but might I also suggest spending the time finding out as much as you can about yourself. Learn about what makes you happy, what you need, what you can live without, what makes sense. You'll need every bit of information no matter what happens, and no matter who you love in this world.

But here's the thing about the love of your life that no one can tell you, the thing that you will have to discover for yourself — the Love part is a verb, not a subject. The *Love of Your Life* is an action, not a person. It's not someone you find who makes you better; it is something you find out how to *do* better. And better. And still better. So keep on loving, love despite the inevitable difficulties and disappointments that come with the territory. And don't stop until you find someone who gets you, laughs at your jokes, smells like home, and kisses you with a passion that's meant for you alone.

And finally, the thing you definitely need to know is this — you belong to a fabulous and long-standing tradition, a tribe of lovers that includes such all-time greats as Walt Whitman, Shakespeare, Michelangelo, Leonardo da Vinci, Abraham Lincoln, Gertrude Stein, Aristotle, Richard Chamberlain (I know. A shock, right?), Tennessee Williams, Marcel Proust, Alvin Ailey, Frank O'Hara, Dusty Springfield, Billie Jean King, Rock Hudson, Freddie Mercury, James Baldwin, Elton John — and that list doesn't include the many gays and lesbians you haven't heard of because, for you, they are yet to be. And though you may sometimes be made to feel *less than* and *outside of* the majority rule, you'll also have plenty of extras to make up for that loss. You will develop a natural understanding of both men and women, because though you are biologically a man, you will want to keep a foot in both camps, while staking a claim in neither. As a result you will be allowed to stand outside and a little away from the crowd, and this will enable you to observe more easily the crazy things that individuals are up to, a valuable asset to you as a writer and an artist. Next year when the senior class casts their production of *Arsenic and Old Lace*, you will be surprised when Doug the Cool offers you the part of Abby Brewster. Naturally you will hesitate, assuming that the invitation is meant as mockery, but curiosity and a chutzpah will win out and you'll accept the challenge. This, as it turns out, will be your greatest triumph. You will be seen, appreciated, and against all odds you will win the respect of every bully who ever laid a hand on you in high school. This experience will embolden you to take chances, and to keep alive in you a healthy skepticism of the mob and the willingness to question, to challenge, and to refuse anything as true until you've tested it yourself.

Oh, and one last thing — remember that book you read, the one that freaked you out because it described homosexuals as a group of men who frequented bowling alley bathrooms and enjoyed putting lightbulbs up each other's asses? Well, it was all wrong, and the author was later discredited and labeled a homophobe. You, as it turns out, are right. Love is everything. Trust your Self. Trust your Life. It will lead you. And so will I . . .

. . . with love,

*James*

# PAULA GILOVICH

*Dear 14,*

I am writing to you from the warped perspective of being thirty-nine years old. This exercise seems to match how strange time is. How it moves like a snake. Exactly what a snake looks like in the grass. Like it is moving quickly. As if it is not moving at all.

You are in a Burger King parking lot. Your makeup is perfect. And by perfect, I mean, bright red lipstick with a darker liner, a pale powder covering up any trace that you are Californian, and heavy thick black eyeliner, which also makes this point. A point against the perpetual sun.

You hang there, out on the concrete, next to cars, next to Xtina. Xtina is a wild girl you have a charge for — your body twitches in her presence. It is the greatest feeling on earth. And because of this charge between you, a wish gets made into the dry air. A wish that — regardless of the dull, dull afternoon — you will live an exceptional life.

And you will.

At fourteen, though, you don't accept this. You don't believe any of this. You discard your strongest thoughts. You change the charge between you and Xtina into something else. You become angry with her for the way she does things. You get angry that she does not keep this nameless thing between the two of you. She flaunts it, or performs it, or exchanges it with complete strangers walking by. And there is the difference right there: For you it is real.

At fourteen, you have thoughts that are unalterable. You might be odder than the oddest types. You have thoughts of being someone new. Or something else. Anything else. Not these people. But you don't think it's okay to say that, especially to these people. At nine, you start drinking Diet Coke, adding a tiny bit of clear alcohol from your parents' collection. It is toxic and disgusting — a great elixir. At twelve you start to avoid the mirror at all costs — closing your eyes in the hallway as you walk by. Praying for some kind of magic disappearing act. Go away, you say. Stay away. And at fourteen where we have arrived, you will do anything a boy asks you to do. And any boy. And none of it matters because you don't feel a thing.

Turns out, though, these details become the very slingshot into a greater life. You move to Seattle. You walk into a feminist, queer-owned sex store. You ask if you can work there. You recognize it as a refuge, a place where queerness thrives, a public space that speaks the truth against all American odds. And it's true, queer is the right place for you. You tell your boyfriend that you are just going to work there a few nights. He understands, but he has no idea you will leave him for all this.

You realize you are queerer than you knew and you start to write with the exact same freedom. It becomes one and the same — who you are and what you write. And you start to live an exceptional life. You write the scripts. You fall in love. You find yourself in the middle of everything you've ever secretly believed in — fearless abandon, warm love, a solid crew, and a life without the mainstream.

You write a play and on closing night, you bat at a half-inflated Mylar balloon, a Warhol balloon, which is part of the set design. The balloon lifts to the ceiling and then rides the air back down. You find it all in one swing. Alone in a black theater, you see your reflection run over several balloons and under many lights. The queerest reflection.

A couple things you should know. All people up close are insane. All lives are bizarre. All people live a life filled with queer thought. That said, however you can do it, earn the freedom to live exactly how you want, and let part of that living be purely of your own invention. Nothing you've ever seen before. And, since you are the ambitious type, spend your life reading the plays and books of the writers collected here. What they have written will topple any kind of resistance to who you want to be.

And always use a condom. I don't care what kind of sex it is.

Sincerely,

*39*

P.S. 14, you do not know anything about sex or how to have it safely. Fourteen-year-olds nowadays can use something called the Internet to find good info on sexuality at www.advocatesforyouth.org. And when they're eighteen, they can go to www.babeland.com for what they need.

# COLMAN DOMINGO

*Dear Colman, the boy in the Grainy Waxy Photograph of 1987,*

Why are you standing with stooped shoulders making that very Bill Cosby-like sweater you are wearing look like it weighs four hundred pounds? I can't tell if you are wearing your sister's hand-me-down sneakers or not because I can only see above your torso in the yearbook photograph. Everyone else seems so glad to have their picture taken for the Overbrook High School newspaper association. You look like you are trying to hide. But how can you? You are tall with high African cheekbones covered with pimply skin. In the photograph you seem to carry shame on top of the weight of that bulky sweater. Shameful secrets. Of catching a whiff of Terrence Jones as he puts you in a headlock between classes. That sweater looks long enough to cover your excitement. Secret thoughts that feel very natural to you, yet forbidden as illustrated on television, in movies, by some woman named Anita Bryant, and pastors from the pulpit, all who tell you that this is far from natural, that it is to be feared, and hated.

Colman, I found that yearbook in the basement storage in your parents' house. I had no idea how it got down there. Maybe it was trying to hide too. I dusted off the pages of the twenty-year-old Overbrook High School Beacon Yearbook. I strained my near-sighted eyes on the grainy black-and-white image of 1987. I smiled at your picture for what seemed like hours. The chasm of then and now filled with memories of all that came after high school and bulky sweaters. Colleges and first loves. Dance parties and gay bars. Twenty years. As I closed the yearbook, I thought I saw your eyes look up and I thought I saw such a dazzling smile part from your lispy lips. And you said to me, "Mmm hmm!" The thought that came to me as I smiled at the grainy photograph was a slogan from the images of Black models dangling Virginia Slims cigarettes from their lips in the 1970s, "You've come a long way, baby!"

My Dearest Colman, I am so glad that we don't cover anything up in bulky sweaters anymore. You dress in fitted clothing and your bulky sweaters are a thing of the sartorial past. Thank God!!! Your secret thoughts are less secret these days and you dress accordingly.

All Yours,

*Colman*

# RICHARD McCANN

Here you are, almost fifty years later, right where I remember you: standing before the bathroom mirror, fretting over the hair wave you have started training, a small, blond, meticulous crest that rises just above your forehead, slicked into place with Brylcreem or Vitalis.

You are eleven years old, a new seventh grader.

Except for occasional unplanned, unhappy glimpses — at the shopping plaza, say, passing a store window — you attempt to confine yourself to looking only in this medicine cabinet mirror, in which you exist as only a face. In this mirror, you can't see your body, heavy and soft and hairless — almost like a girl's, you think. You've read about Christine Jorgensen, the man who went to Denmark to have an operation that turned him into a woman, and seen her Before and After photos in *Life* magazine.

Maybe you're like her, you worry. How else to explain what feels so unspeakable about you? And I wish you felt this as a question, rather than a worry. There is no right answer, no "explanation" necessary for any of the feelings you have right now that seem so unspeakable.

Your mother taps on the bathroom door. "Are you all right in there?"

In the months since your father's death, she has begun to watch you more closely. She has taken to telling you that your father had confided in her before he died that he was worried that you played too much with girls. She says you need what she calls "male influence."

But you keep studying your hair, pushing at it with your plastic comb. *If I can just get my hair right,* you keep thinking, *I'll be all right too.* There's not too much to praise about you. But people have told you that you have nice hair.

As for me, your older self: I'm standing behind you, though you can't see me. But even if you could, you'd never turn to say hello. You wouldn't want to hear a single word that I might have to say.

And why would you? I'm the homosexual our mother has warned you about.

If you were looking for me you'd be looking for a man in a white Cadillac, the one who supposedly offers rides to boys like you; or the man some kid once saw lurking by the creek down the hill from the schoolyard. And of course that man is a myth. But how else would you recognize me except through the stories you've already learned about men like me, the kind of man you hope never to become? I may as well be one of those inverts you once saw pictured in an old psychology book, five or six of them lined up against the bare concrete wall of a mental institution, their eyes masked with thick black lines, as if to grant them some modesty that they didn't really deserve. You already understood, however, that those black lines covering their eyes were actually meant to protect the viewer from the awful sickness of their gazes.

There is much I'd like to tell you, if you were able to listen. I'd like to tell you that you'll find love. That you'll find true family among your dear, astonishing friends. That the world is larger and far different than anything you can yet imagine.

But you're not ready to hear any of this.

You're worried about your hair. You're worried about school, where you wander the long corridors alone.

Even now, standing so close, it seems there is nothing I can do but wait for you to come forward, a heavy, unhappy child, and begin your long walk through the years ahead toward me. There's nothing I can do but stand here, bearing toward you an affection that you cannot yet even begin to imagine offering yourself.

# MARION DANE BAUER

*To my dear young Marion,*

How glad I am to reach back to that long-ago girl to acknowledge your existence, perhaps even to offer a bit of advice. But *which* young Marion should I speak to?

The eleven-year-old who, in 1950, changed to a new school to escape the snide girls who made her life a daily misery . . . only to find that misery compounded. "If you are the problem," you said to yourself, filled with a new sad wisdom, "moving doesn't help, because you take yourself with you." But still, you had no idea *why* you were the problem.

The thirteen-year-old who used to check her clothes on Tuesdays and Thursdays to make sure she wasn't wearing yellow or green, the certain mark of a fairy? Did you know what a fairy was? You must have. Mostly, though, you knew that being a fairy was bad . . . bad beyond imagining.

The sixteen-year-old who waited to be invited back to her summer job at St. Mary's Episcopal Girls' Camp . . . and waited and waited? Your roommate waited too. The invitation never came. You were, you knew, the two best counselors the sisters had at that camp, but you were also something else that neither of you dared name. As innocent as your relationship was — and it was as innocent as two rule-abiding adolescent girls in love with each other could possibly be in 1955 — you were filled with shame at your silent dismissal.

The twenty-year-old who walked down the aisle of her childhood church to do what she knew she was supposed to do, marry a man? What did it matter that you knew you didn't want him? "Till death do us part!" You made that vow with particular vehemence because you already understood you were going to have to hold yourself to it with every ounce of energy you could muster. And muster you did . . . for twenty-eight long years.

What advice do I have for that girl caught in a time when her deepest impulse toward love wasn't acceptable to her family, to her friends, to her church, to her society, to the psychologists who handed down dictums about what was healthy and what — in their all-powerful certainty - was not? I find myself stymied. What can I say? The culture in which I grew up seems to obliterate all attempts at passing down wisdom into that time. Perhaps, though, a peek into the future, your future, will serve better than any advice.

The friendless eleven-year-old will grow past being eleven and being miserable and being awkward. And yes, she will have friends, many friends. Some will share her "difference," many will not, but all will accept her exactly as she is. She will learn social skills she didn't have at eleven. Especially, she will learn to listen and to care about the stories that make up other people's lives. And that listening, that caring will bring her friends.

The older she grows, the wider her community will be too, and the easier it will be to find people she likes and who like her. She will move to a city where she will find a thriving lesbian community. She will join a church that supports lesbian, gay, bisexual, and transgender people unequivocally. She will find a love that comforts and nurtures every single day. And she will come to understand that she doesn't need affection or even approval from every person she meets.

The thirteen-year-old struggling over her wardrobe will learn to be who she is, wear what she feels good in, and let other people's problems be theirs.

We all have to abide by certain rules about our dress unless we want to stir up a lot of fuss. But these days I decide for myself what I want my clothes to say. Most of the time my partner and I wear what is, I suppose, the uniform for aging dykes, jeans and T-shirts. That is our choice, not because it's the uniform but because jeans and T-shirts are practical, comfortable, and economical. But still I love putting on a long skirt and a silky blouse and going into the world as that other part of this woman I am. And I love knowing that such choices are mine, no one else's.

The sixteen-year-old who lost a job for a love she had not even dared name will find many doors in her life.

I was forty-seven years old before I had the courage and the insight to acknowledge my sexuality — even to myself — and to make the choices appropriate to what I finally understood. A few years later I edited and contributed to a collection of gay and lesbian short stories called *Am I Blue? Coming Out from the Silence.* As I was finishing the manuscript, an editor I had worked with for many years asked, "You aren't coming out in that book, are you?" When I said I was, he was deeply concerned for my career. Another editor asked the same question and, getting the same answer, hesitated for a moment, then said, "Well . . . for every door that will be closed I'm sure another will be opened." And that is the way it has been. Some doors may have closed, but others have opened and opened and opened. I have learned that being honest with myself and others, even and especially when that honesty comes hard, is its own reward.

The twenty-year-old marrying without a trace of desire will learn that she, inevitably, makes mistakes and that even mistakes can bring great gifts. My marriage gave me two children and now a passel of grandchildren, and I *wanted* those children and those grandchildren with all my soul. Lesbians can adopt these days or even conceive, but in the 1960s, without my poorly chosen marriage, children would have been denied completely. That marriage also gave me a secure foundation from which I could develop my career during the long years before I could actually support myself with my writing. Would I have chosen a different life if I had known myself better? Of course. Do I regret the choices I made? There is no point. I just keep making choices, sometimes making mistakes, and living, day by day.

So what do I have to offer as advice for the girl I was and for those who will come after me? Only this: You will find love and you will struggle with that love as all humans do, but in that struggle will come a discovery that, at your very core, you are precisely who you are meant to be. In that understanding lies the beginnings of an honorable and healthy and enormously satisfying life.

Your capacity to love is your greatest strength and the greatest gift you have to bring to the world.

Live it. Rejoice in it.

Live and rejoice in yourself!

In gratitude for resilience and for the more open world I have grown into at age seventy-two,

*Marion*

# LUCY THURBER

*Dear Lucy,*

Right now you are thirteen years old, almost fourteen. Your body is changing: You have breasts, hips, and you don't recognize yourself. You can't run like you used to; your breasts get in the way, and your thighs, which have always been compact and muscular, have weight on them. It feels like your body is dragging you down.

You feel empty all the time. And you want things, big scary things. You can't even say what they are because you don't know the words for it, or how to give it a name. And you've started to have dreams about girls — dreams about kissing them, dreams about touching them. You wake up frightened. You wake up turned on. You wake up disgusted with yourself.

You go to school. You feel weird in your body — too big, hulking. You're different from everyone and you know it. They know it too. They smell it on you. It's more than the fact that you read too much and talk too much in class. It's more than the fact that you're poor, that your clothes, your hair, your shoes don't match the rest of the kids. It's something more. You feel like you're wrong somehow.

You walk down the school halls and you see the girls you dream about. It feels strange to see them in real life because the dreams are so real. And in your dreams, their mouths, their hands, their words have been so intimate. You feel like you know them and they know you, but they don't. And maybe nobody knows you, because sometimes you think there is something evil in you, something rotten because of the things you want, the things you are too terrified to name.

And, Lucy, you are lonely. You are so lonely you can hardly breathe. You want to be touched, kissed, held — you want to be loved and it seems impossible. Impossible that you will ever find the words to speak all the things inside you, speak all your longing, all your fear. You think you will drown in your longing. You're terrified you're just going to disappear.

But here is what is really going to happen: You will wait. It will be almost like fasting, the waiting, because you will be starving for love, starving to be seen. But you will find things to sustain you. You will read. You will write. You will listen to music. You will go to the movies. You will find a friend or a teacher or a coach who sees you and is brave like you. You will discover theater and the beautiful freedom of make-believe. You will invest in your imagination, in the power of telling and listening to stories. You will start to see that your story fits into the larger human story. You will know that your voice is important, and that you have something to say. And then, when you're old enough, you will leave.

You will go to a big city and it will be bright, dirty, and you will be free. You will find your people and they will love you. They will see you, and when they do, all the things inside you, the things you think are ugly, dark, and rotten — they will call them beautiful, glorious, and wonderful. You will finally be kissed, held, and loved. It will be very romantic. And the want in you, the unnamable desire — one day you will just say it, name it, know it. You will say, "Oh, it's so simple, I'm gay," and you will be so, so happy about it. You won't be alone. I promise you. I know, because I am you.

Love,

*Lucy*

# RANDALL KENAN

*Dear Garrett,*

Don't be blue. Despite how you feel sometimes, you really don't have a lot to be blue about. True, you're a poor country boy from the swamps of North Carolina. But, as improbable as it may seem, where you come from will become one of your greatest assets as a human being.

Look at everything. Remember everything. Observe everything from what it's like to be in a tobacco field in the July heat, to the old women at First Baptist in their Sunday-go-to-Meeting hats and the rhythm of the Deacons' prayers. Remember that feeling like lightning shooting through your arteries when you walk up on a rattlesnake. Remember the argument you had with Mrs. Johnson about your overwritten basketball article in the school paper. Remember the funerals and the band practices and the nights you spent with the EMTs at the Fire and Rescue squad. Everything is important.

Keep reading the dictionary for fun. When people make fun of you, just keep on doing what you're doing. You've got the right idea. However, dropping $150 words in casual conversation is not always a great idea. It makes you look like a smart-ass know-it-all. You are a smart-ass know-it-all, but you don't have to let everybody know it, just your family and closest friends. Remember they love you despite your faults. This fact will be important. Physics, science fiction, classical music — if you're interested, keep on studying it. Don't let anybody tell you it's a waste of time or not something a black kid should be interested in. All your peers who think that basketball is the end-all-and-be-all of the Universe; all those folks who sneer at standard English and who think only "sissies" believe in subject and verb agreement — leave them to their own devices. Don't ever worry about being "black enough" for anybody. You will learn, soon enough, that black folks have been at the foundations of all human experience: Nothing human is alien to you and your people, despite what the television and movies and magazines try to shove down your throat. You are not merely an "honorary Negro." Your ancestors paid that bill for you a long time ago.

You grew up in the Church and right now the Church is strong with you. You worry about your so-called "unnatural affections" and the Scriptures and what Jesus thinks. Despite what people say, to quote one of your favorite songs in a few years, "The Lord don't mind." It's foolish to think that any type of loving is wrong. That cat, Jesus, was all about love. So please don't waste time focusing on the species of love but the quality of the love. Keep studying theology; it will come in handy later in a strange and wonderful way. (Please note: I said theology, not religion.)

You were born rich in identity — Black, Southern, Queer. Don't ever let anybody tell you any bit of it is a burden. The sooner you start seeing your background, your reality, as a diamond mine, the sooner you will see yourself as a force to be reckoned with. In fact, though you don't know it, you are a force already — just don't mention it in casual conversation. That would be a little obnoxious. Just *be* a force. "O to be a dragon!" (The woman who wrote that, Miss Marianne Moore, will become one of your favorite poets. I envy the feeling you will get the first time you encounter her poems.)

The world is going to change in many ways for the better for black folk and for queer folk. However, ways of looking at black men, despite our achievements and accomplishments in the great world, will remain a vexed thing. So much of how the culture-at-large looks at black men, and their view of what a "man" should be is pure fantasy. A lot of this claptrap is designed to hurt you and to cut you down. To keep you in a box. To tell you what you should and should not do. Later for all that noise, brother.

And how this country looks at queer black men, in particular — well, I hate to tell you but you'll still be a strange and exotic creature in the eyes of a great many Americans. Big deal. Do not waste a minute fretting over how they look upon you. You have the power to define yourself — remember that power; take that control. It's like a superpower, really, to be whom you want to be, to do what you want to do, to fly where you want to fly. Your life will get more complicated, but think of it as a great adventure, every damn day. You're going to have fun.

Fun is waiting for you to have it.

Oh, and get this book and read it: *The Art of Worldly Wisdom* by Baltasar Gracián. I didn't discover it until I was thirty-one, and I wish I'd read it when I was your age. It can help you through some dark moments.

Don't smoke. Pay your taxes. Be wise in matters of sex and your body — a plague is coming: You can and will survive it, though the casualties will break your heart. Just keep creating.

And please buy lots of Apple stock. You'll thank me. And I don't mean the Beatle's music company either. Leave that to Michael Jackson. Trust me.

For I remain,

*Your loving self*

248

# JAYE MAIMAN

*Dear Janice,*

I imagine this letter finds you on a gloomy day. So many of your days are overcast, clouded by your insecurities, fears, and doubts. Today I find you in one of your refuges. There you are, sitting on the beach at the edge of Sea Gate in Brooklyn — a private, gated community of which you are not part. You've snuck past a torn fence and found an odd boulder, the size of a Ford pickup truck, aggregated from concrete, sand, shells, and soda cans. You climb on top and wait patiently for the waves to lap around you, creating an island for you.

How many of your stormy ruminations stem from your deepening awareness that you are different? And do you recognize where that sense of difference originates?

Later that night, you sit in a dark theater in Coney Island, not far from the misfits and carnival games on the boardwalk. You can feel the gentle summer heat rising from either side of you, from the suntanned skin of your father, a gentle giant who reminds you of John Wayne, and from your mother, whose cool hand tightly clasps yours. There, cuddled together and apart from your parents, you dream of being James Bond rescuing damsels in distress, and whisper to yourself: I like women.

Still, you do not connect that soul-shrinking clench of being different with these revelations. You just feel that awful sense of otherness and peer out at those around you as if from the far side of a riverbank. It's as if you — strolling along the promenade by the Verrazano Bridge — could somehow sense that the place you will really find yourself and build your own family is *out there*, on the fogged-in banks of New Jersey, where one day, astonishingly, you will live with your wife and children.

You should know that the sense of being an outsider will change with time. There are gifts being born in this very moment of isolation that will eventually become your greatest strengths. You are discovering a clarity of sight, an ability to listen and hear the undercurrents of conversation, to read the space between words. You are learning the art of empathy, how your heart can unfold to let in the small and large suffering of people who cannot give voice to their pain. In your distance from the people you encounter every day, you are unconsciously calculating ways to construct bridges for you to reach them, for them to discover you. Because, although you have not yet stumbled onto this awareness, what you crave most is connection. Love.

At the same time, knowing all this would not release you from the grip of the dark emotions that caused you once to step over the outside rails of your tenth-floor apartment terrace and speculate, what would it be like to let go? These moments of despair you guard fiercely. You are the good child, the good student, the quiet one who does what is expected and what is right and never asks for anything from anyone. Your mother dubs you "The Rock," which in midnight hours causes you to weep silently into your pillow.

The Rock is impenetrable. Unknowable. In your heart, you fear that if you were revealed, if you were really seen, your loneliness would explode your world.

At the local pizzeria across the corner from Lincoln High School, where you could get two slices and a soda for a dollar, teenagers gather in tight clutches of gossip, and chatter about their crushes. You shrink away to avoid their inquiries.

Watching television with your parents, strolling with shoulders hunched through the local park, you spin daydreams of a loving future, but they never include you. The only way to imagine happiness is by creating stories in which a man and woman fall into love, and somehow, vaguely, confusingly, you are always able to create the romancing male with so much more vividness than you do the pursued female.

How shocked you would be to hear that you will one day exchange vows with a woman, in front of a rabbi, beneath a rainbow chuppah, with your proud parents, family, friends, and work colleagues rejoicing at your pronouncement of love. That this commitment ceremony would be followed by the births of your son and daughter would strike you as a prospect less likely than the world ending with Charlton Heston howling over the buried remnants of the Statue of Liberty.

From this future that I inhabit, which your fantasies could never have envisioned, I tell you this: You will be happy. Those simple words, that proclamation, would have left you breathless.

Your path will not be easy. But oddly, with every challenge, you will discover new strengths, new confidence, and deeper joy. You will also discover that some hurdles are your own creations, and they will evaporate as soon as you have the guts to test them.

The opening comes one day with a friend who lives in your apartment building. She sports short curly hair, with sprinkles of gray amidst the black despite her teen years, and her eyes have a sparkle you've never seen before. She is as light and as surprising as a fern growing out of crevices of a cracked brownstone. She laughs so easily, it seems to you for the first time that perhaps you could find another way of being. You begin testing her, to see if knowing you, *really* knowing you, would cause her to retreat.

Sitting in her darkened bedroom on one of your many sleep-overs, with shadows flickering on the wall from the television in the living room where her parents have fallen asleep watching Johnny Carson, you expose the blackest of your thoughts. In the pale light, you catch her eye and are taken aback when she listens and does not retreat. Eventually, you will risk letting her know that you suspect you are a lesbian. And the friendship will remain unmovable. But you tread carefully nonetheless, terrified that if you focus too much on this way of being different, you would lose this anchor in your life. You focus instead on ways to hold on to this lifeline.

In time, she teaches you to laugh. You aren't really sure how this happens. Over the years, you watch her sing off-key songs with her brother without an ounce of self-consciousness, or joke with her father over the bag he brought home from the deli, or discover humor in the way two people bumped in the hallway. You won't understand how profoundly this lesson will impact you. Laughter offered you planks with which you could begin to build bridges, to find connections, to show others: I am different, and yet through humor, you and I can find what it is that we have in common.

In high school, you fall in love for the first time. Your bubble of isolation now grows large enough to include someone else as invested in hiding as you are. Your friend's father goes in for heart surgery and you, good friend that you are, stay with her for weeks, alone in her apartment, playing house and closing out the world.

The two of you will be teased mercilessly by others who suspect that your relationship is more than just friendship. They sing Charlie Rich's "When You Get Behind Closed Doors" as you pass in the halls. At your thirtieth high school reunion, many of those same unrelenting girls will reveal that they later came out themselves, after failed marriages and hard journeys of their own.

She will break your heart one day, leaving you in one of the most stereotypical scenarios. An affair with the gym teacher. You cannot talk with anyone about how much you ache, how devastated you feel by her betrayal. But from my wonderful vantage point, I would urge you to turn around and shift your perspective back to the glimpse of bliss you discovered with her, behind closed doors. If only you could have recognized that this first relationship was a hint, a promise of what was to come. Here is what is to come. Here is what I wish you could have seen when you looked over the railing in Brooklyn, when you sat alone on your boulder in Sea Gate.

You will come out to your mother, who will be singularly unimpressed and remind you that you can nonetheless have children. Your uncle will tell you that he was not surprised since only another woman could truly appreciate an intelligent woman. You will cease using indefinite nouns at work to refer to your partners, which amazingly none of your colleagues ever questioned or confronted. You will publish a series of lesbian mysteries, and when the first one is printed and displayed at A Different Light, your John Wayne–sized father, who looked like he could have been cutting down logs or fishing with rednecks, would shout out in the front of the store, "That's my daughter's book!" At work, you will come out and advocate for benefits for gay couples, and become a role model for young gay professionals. You will build an astonishing chosen family of gay friends. You will find more connections than you have time to manage.

And you will spend decades with the woman you never dared dream of, raising wonderful children you weren't capable of imagining in a century-old home in New Jersey, which in itself would have made you laugh. And you didn't have to become James Bond to achieve anything of these wonderful moments. You just had to be yourself.

Love,
*Jaye*

# DAVID LEAVITT

*Letter at Fifty to the Self Who at Twenty-Five Wrote a Letter to His Thirteen-Year-Old Self Assuring Him that Everything Would Be OK*

*Dear Self,*

Everything you hope for — companionship, stability, a house, a dog — will come true.

Everything you fear — loss, confusion, panic, emptiness — will come true.

It will dawn on you that what you hope for and what you fear are inextricable.

You will be astonished to discover that you have lived with the same person for twenty years.

You will be more astonished to discover that you can now marry this person but only if you move to another state.

You will be even more astonished to discover that you and this person share the view that you would not get married even if you did move to another state, that you would rather live together in sin like the hippie couples you knew when you were growing up.

What repulses you at twenty-five — gay men referring to each other as "she" — you will practice (but with a sense of irony).

What enthralls you at twenty-five but repulsed you at thirteen — anonymous, animalistic sex — you will look back on with nostalgia.

Success will cease to be your primary goal.

You will give up on hoping that the world will get better.

The world will get better.

The world will get worse.

You will find it impossible to believe that you have lived this long.

You would not want to be twenty-five again, or thirteen again, for anything in the world.


*The Earlier Letter (excerpted from the novel* Equal Affections)


Danny's fantasy: He is twelve years old, riding his bicycle to the shopping mall to read soap opera magazines. A sunny Saturday afternoon, the shopping mall quiet, full of women in tennis dresses and plump teenage girls, their stomachs bulging out of stiff jeans, who've come here in gangs to smoke. Danny is wearing shorts, a T-shirt emblazoned with the name of the university where his father teaches, tube socks, tennis shoes. His legs are brown from the sun, the hairs on them bleached white. He is locking his bicycle to a lamppost, unscrambling the combination with dirty fingers, when he feels the proximity of another body, feels warm breath against his hair. He turns around, still crouched, and a man is standing over him, a tall man in a gray leather jacket and jeans, a man who is at once a stranger and oddly, intimately familiar to him — but where from? A student of his father's? A cousin he doesn't remember? "Excuse me," the man says, "I'm sorry to bother you, I —" He puts his hands in his pockets, looks away. "Danny," he says. "Danny."

Danny's eyes suddenly fill with tears. His cheeks flush. He looks at the ground.

"I'm you," the stranger says. "I'm who you're going to become. And I've come to tell you — to reassure you — you're going to be fine, just fine."

The boy stands. Of course he sees it now, all of it — that face so familiar because it is his own, but also so strange, because he's never seen his own face before, not really, except in a mirror, and now he understands how mirrors distort, and where his legs will stretch to, and the awkward unpuzzling of his own face. Tears are welling in his eyes, and in his grown self's eyes as well, as the man bends down, leans over him, puts a hand on his shoulder. "All the things you're worried about," he says, "all the things that make you suffer — they're nothing. They're smoke. I know. And I've come so you'll know, so you won't have to suffer anymore. For you're going to be fine. You're going to leave California and head East, just like you hope. And you'll have love, Danny. I know you can't believe it now, I know everything you feel. You don't imagine anyone will ever love you, you can't conceive how anyone could love you. But someone will. You'll see."

The hand on his shoulder — larger, thickly veined, bristled with short brown hairs — is his own hand. Young Danny, crouching still by his bicycle, runs his own fingers over those long fingers, feels the warmth of the skin. One after the other he traces them, until his hand comes to rest on the slender silver ring. Slowly he strokes the ring's rounded outer edge; slowly he rotates it around the finger on which it's lodged. Under the ring is a perfect white band where the skin has not been touched by the sun.

# DAVID EBERSHOFF

*Letter Home*
*July 2011—July 1984*

*Dear David,*

Let's get a few things out of the way. Yes, you have a boyfriend. No, he isn't a professional tennis player. Yes, you own a car. No, it isn't a black Rabbit convertible. Yes, you got into college. No, it wasn't Princeton — but that wouldn't have been the right place for you. Yes, everyone knows you're gay. No, people didn't freak out. Most people already knew anyway.

The other day I was on my yoga mat — I know, yoga; I didn't see that one coming either — when I thought of you in that long hot summer of 1984 when you never felt more alone. A few things came to mind: your corduroy Op shorts growing loose on your waist because you were too anxious to eat; the round tortoiseshell glasses always smudged with fingerprints; and the red Schwinn bicycle you rode all over Pasadena just to escape your life. It's been a while since I thought of you behind your bedroom door moaning with the Smiths ("How Soon Is Now?") and the Thompson Twins ("Hold Me Now"). I was trying to figure out what you might want to hear from me in the future — what I could possibly say that Morrissey wasn't already teaching you. After all, what is more trenchant, and true, than *I am human and I need to be loved, just like everybody else does.*

There's this slogan going around these days — It Gets Better. While that's mostly true — being gay gets better, or at least easier — I realized those words wouldn't completely resonate with you. You've never been one for pick-me-ups or complex feelings boiled down to catchphrases. Your skepticism of the trendy is admirable (if a bit trendy itself). Anyway, here's what I want you to know, and I hope you take this the right way: Stop waiting for the future because the person you are today is in many ways the person you will be.

And that's the good news!

I'm not saying you won't evolve. I'm not saying your life won't improve. I'm not saying that the sucky parts of being David E — the tortured shyness, the alone-ness, the back acne — won't abate. What I'm saying is this: If you want to save yourself a lot of time and get on with the business of living happily, you might want to understand yourself a little better now. The best parts of who you are today will affect who you'll become — can become, I should say. Yes, part of this is about being gay and coming to love yourself. That's important — essential, in fact. But I'm actually talking about something larger. I'm talking about your core beliefs. The things and principles you most value in life. I know you roll your eyes at words like values and beliefs and principles. See, there they go turning behind your glasses. (Sidebar: In a few years you'll give up the goggles for contact lenses.) The reason these words make you cynical is because you've heard them primarily from the mouths of cynical people whom you rightly distrust — the hateful preachers, lying politicians, anyone who says you are wrong or *less* because you keep crushing on boys. (Another sidebar: no need to waste your entire senior year hearting after Jeff. He isn't gay, and tucking anonymous notes under his windshield wiper isn't going to change that.) Those people say they are talking about values and principles and beliefs — but they aren't. You already know this.

But what you don't know, or at least haven't yet articulated to yourself, is that you have strong — very strong — values and principles and beliefs yourself. These beliefs will guide you for the rest of your life, if you let them. If you don't ignore them. If you refuse to let others diminish them. These beliefs already help define who you are. If you hang on to them and don't let them get muddled up in ideas that aren't important to you, they will guide you to the best version of yourself, which is just another way of saying leading a happy life.

Take for example your belief in words.

You love to read. Eudora Welty, with her cat's-eye glasses and the hump atop her spine, is your hero. *The Stranger* terrified you, although you're not sure why. You giggled along with Jane Austen, thinking you were the only one getting her irony. And *Wuthering Heights* revealed a storm in your heart that will never really go away. Guess what — this profound connection with books isn't going to change. In fact, that's going to be a core part of who you are. It will be a big part of how the world knows you. Through words and books. I know that seems unlikely for a boy from the smoggy suburbs of Los Angeles, but it's true. It will only become true, however, once you ask yourself directly and sincerely what you truly believe in. For some reason, I didn't ask that question of myself until I was in my mid-twenties, despite the powerful feelings books created in me. Had I asked it when I was your age I would have been able to answer it, because the answer was already there.

Look, I know this summer feels eternal. There's a heat wave. And a smog alert. It's too hot to be outside and yet every day your mom, before she leaves for work, tells you to go out and *do something*. But what? You don't have any plans except the daily training for cross-country. You don't have a job. You don't have a driver's license. And, let's face it, you don't have many friends. Yet as drifting as this summer feels, in fact it's turning into a great project that will forever shape you. Don't believe me? Ask yourself how you've spent your days. That's right, reading. Devouring books like they were food.

When you were younger, whenever you complained about being bored your mom would say, "Read a book." That's what you've been doing this summer, almost a book a day. Except this is the summer you discovered that the Pasadena Public Library — yes, conservative old Pasadena — carries gay books. Books that are either about men who love men like *A Boy's Own Story*, *Maurice*, *Giovanni's Room*, or books like the plays of Tennessee Williams and *Other Voices, Other Rooms* that have a gay sensibility that you recognize. You've been inhaling these books for weeks, each one shoring up your own belief in yourself. You've fallen into a summer routine. You get up and ride to the Pasadena Public Library and find a book that has anything to do with gay and take it to a quiet corner and read all day. You don't dare check it out because that would leave a record of your instincts. Most of the time you finish before you have to go home for dinner. When you don't, you hide the book on a remote shelf so that you won't have to encounter a librarian over re-shelving and reserving. The next day you return to keep reading. Again and again and again. This is how you discover Thomas Mann and Carson McCullers and Joe Orton. How you first read Armistead Maupin and Rita Mae Brown. How you met the words of a writer you'll always revere, Edmund White.

One day not long ago something unlikely happened. You ran out of gay books. You read your way through the library's limited collection of queer. Your discreet search of the card catalog turned up nothing new. You weren't brave enough to ask the librarian for a suggestion. Instead you rode the red Schwinn over to the Pasadena Plaza. On the mall's second floor you hunted around Waldenbooks until you found the small gay and lesbian section at the back of the store, next to health and fitness with that oversized exercise book called *Buns!* staring at you. Trembling, you bought your first gay book, *Forgetting Elena* by Edmund White, with the money you earned babysitting Friday and Saturday nights for the past two years. Back in your bedroom you read it in an afternoon. Though you barely understood it, its mood of longing felt exactly how you've been feeling all summer — the hot sun, the hypersensitivity to male flesh, the endless cycle of longing and hunting and devouring.

Now you have a new routine: up in the morning, on the Schwinn, and over to Walden for another book. Today, it's *Family Dancing* by David Leavitt, the Warner mass market paperback with wet footprints on the cover. You buy the book, frightened the clerk will figure you out (in fact, he's too stoned to care) and bicycle home in something of a trance, the little plastic Walden bag dangling from your wrist. The house is empty and you run to your room and fling yourself on your bed and begin to read. And read and read and read. These stories are about young gay men from middle-class families in California — men who could be you in a few years! How much you recognize — the swimming pools and the mothers who drive station wagons and sunbathe in bikinis and cocoa butter and their sons who break from the family in search of love. All of it feels like you.

No one will be home until 4:30 or 5:00, but you must read quickly. You don't stop to eat. You don't stop to do anything except maybe pee. You don't want to stop because this summer, for the first time, you are seeing evidence of yourself beyond yourself, if you know what I mean. Evidence in black ink and cheap mass market pulp that your existence is worthy of print. Proof that you're not alone in this cyclone of feelings. It's late July and you've been doing this for two weeks now, maybe ten books bought and read in this adolescent fever dream of words. You don't pause to analyze the books or their layers of meaning. All you want from them is what they mean to you. The recognition of emotions. The recognition of impulses. The mirror on the page. All you are doing is reading and feeling and you've never felt more free. The words are saving you from yourself.

At around 3:30, with the thought of Mom pulling up the driveway in her paneled estate wagon, you finish the book. Another day and another book and another day of inching closer to a kind of love you've never felt before — a love for these words, for these pages, and, eventually, yourself. Although you love the book in your hand, although the last five hours of your life disappeared because of the words on these pages, you also know you must get rid of the book. You are fifteen. You aren't prepared for the world to know that this is what you love — that the great loves of your life will have to do with *this*. Men and words. Loving men and loving words. That these are your great passions and they will always be intertwined somehow. With each passing day, and each new book, you come closer to understanding this. Still, you can't let anyone know this and so you must get rid of the evidence: the book. It can't sit on your shelf. In your heart, yes. But not on your shelf.

When they say it gets better, for you, David, this is what that means. After this long summer you will never again have to do what you're about to do. You take *Family Dancing* outside behind the garage. You drop it into an empty aluminum trash bin. You look at it, at the paperback cover you held so tightly that it's now creased, and you douse it in Kingsford lighter fluid (from one of those metal squeezable cans). You open a matchbook pocketed at Ariba! (your mom's favorite Mexican restaurant) and you drop the small flame into the can. You burn the book you just read. You get rid of it. You watch the flames eat the words — just as you ate the words all day — until they are no more. Not only are you eliminating your greatest love, you are destroying evidence of it. For no one must know that you are drawn to stories about men who love each other. That you long to read more stories like this, and one day write them too. You poke the black pages with a stick until they are ash. Then you throw a little dirt into the bin and go back to your room. You did this two weeks ago with *Forgetting Elena* and you did this yesterday with *Dancer from the Dance* and you'll do it tomorrow and I'm writing you today to tell you after this summer you'll never do this again.

Here's the miracle: those words you burned in the trash bin? They're still with you. Not verbatim, of course. But the feelings they created have stayed for almost thirty years. You can't know this now, but this hot summer of books is creating your future. Your love of books will become so great that you will create a life around them. You will become a writer, an editor, a teacher. All of it about words. You will have many friends, and a couple of boyfriends, who come into your life because of words. Your happiest hours will be when you are working to find the right words. You will become a professional word nerd not because of career ambition but because of the love those books this summer have given you.

That's what I want you to know. Yes, your life will change. Yes, things will get better. Yes, that feeling of being trapped will go away. But not everything will change, thankfully. I want you to notice what you love the most right now, today — for this will guide you a long, long way.

Love,
*David*

# ACKNOWLEDGMENTS

All my thanks to: James Lecesne, for his lovely partnership in this project; Arthur Levine, for being so very good at his job; Matt Hudson; the authors who said yes (and made their friends say yes) when this book was just an idea; my loving, funny family; Amy Bloom and her extraordinary talent as both a writer and a mother; students and colleagues at Saint Ann's School; Alexis Waller, Priscilla Swan, Margaret Goodwin, Ellen Shapiro, Paula Gilovich, Kate Roberts, Annie Rollyson, Max MacMillan, Claire Mannle; Jasmine, for her reading and re-reading, wisecracking, title-creating, typo-spotting, and love supreme.

SARAH MOON

I want to thank The Trevor Project and all the people who work so hard to support LGBT and Questioning youth throughout the U.S. I am especially grateful to my fellow co-founders, Peggy Rajski and Randy Stone. And as always, my thanks to Bill Clegg for standing by me.

JAMES LECESNE

# CONTRIBUTORS

**LaShonda Katrice Barnett** is the author of the short story collection *Callaloo* and editor of *I Got Thunder: Black Women Songwriters on Their Craft*. Her stories have appeared in numerous queer anthologies including *Does Your Mama Know?*, *Homestretch: Chasing the American Dyke Dream*, and *Hot & Bothered* volumes I, II, and III.

**Marion Dane Bauer** is the author of over eighty books, including the 1987 Newbery Honor Book *On My Honor*. She was the editor and a contributor to the groundbreaking collection of gay- and lesbian-themed short stories *Am I Blue? Coming Out from the Silence*.

**Lucy Jane Bledsoe** is the author of four novels, a collection of short fiction, a collection of narrative nonfiction, and six books for kids.

**Amy Bloom** is the author of three short story collections, two novels, one children's book, and a book of essays on gender and culture. Her work has been published in fifteen countries and nominated for the National Book Award and the National Book Critics Circle Award. She received the National Magazine Award for Fiction.

**Anne Bogart** is the Artistic Director of SITI Company, which she founded with Japanese director Tadashi Suzuki in 1992. She is a recipient of two OBIE Awards, a Bessie Award, a Guggenheim as well as a Rockefeller Fellowship, a USA Artists Fellow, and is a professor at Columbia University where she runs the Graduate Directing Program.

**Paige Braddock** is the Creative Director at Charles M. Schulz's studio in Santa Rosa, California. Paige is the creator of the comic *Jane's World* and co-creator of the graphic novel *The Martian Confederacy*.

**Melanie Braverman** is the author of the novel *East Justice* (Permanent Press, 1996) and the poetry collection *Red* (Perugia Press, 2002), winner of the Publishing Triangle's Audre Lorde Poetry Prize. She is Poet-in-Residence at Brandeis University.

**Nick Burd** attended the University of Iowa and received his MFA from the New School. The *New York Times Book Review* named his debut novel, *The Vast Fields of Ordinary*, a Notable Book of 2009. Nick's second book from Dial Books for Young Readers is forthcoming.

Cartoonist **Jennifer Camper**'s books include *Rude Girls and Dangerous Women* and *subGURLZ*, and she is the editor of two Juicy Mother comix anthologies. Her cartoons and illustrations have appeared in magazines, newspapers, comic books, and anthologies, and have been exhibited internationally. www.jennifercamper.com

**Bill Clegg** is the author of the memoirs *Portrait of an Addict as a Young Man* and *Ninety Days*. He is a literary agent in New York City.

**Bruce Coville** has received over a dozen Children's Choice Awards, and has written more than a hundred books for young people, including *My Teacher Is an Alien* and *Into the Land of the Unicorns*. He runs an audiobook company called Full Cast Audio and lives in Syracuse, New York, with his wife, Katherine.

**Howard Cruse** was the founding editor of *Gay Comix* in 1980 and the creator in 1983 of the *Wendel* comic strip series for the *Advocate*.

He has published nine books, including the critically acclaimed and international award-winning graphic novel *Stuck Rubber Baby*.

**Michael Cunningham** is the author of the novels *A Home at the End of the World, Flesh and Blood, The Hours* (winner of the PEN/Faulkner Award and the Pulitzer Prize), and *Specimen Days*. He lives in New York.

**Ray Daniels** received an MFA in Creative Writing from Warren Wilson College and is currently a teacher, writer, and freelance editor.

**Benoit Denizet-Lewis** is an award-winning contributing writer for the *New York Times Magazine*. Formerly a senior writer at *Boston Magazine* and staff writer at the *San Francisco Chronicle*, his work has also appeared in *Sports Illustrated, Details, Slate, Spin, Out*, and others.

**Stacey D'Erasmo**'s first novel, *Tea*, was selected as a *New York Times* Notable Book. Her second novel, *A Seahorse Year*, was named a Best Book of the Year by the *San Francisco Chronicle* and *Newsday* and won both a Lambda Literary Award and a Ferro-Grumley Award. Her third novel, *The Sky Below*, was published by Houghton Mifflin Harcourt.

**Carole DeSanti** is an acquisitions editor at Viking Penguin, known for her championing of independent, original voices in women's fiction. She is also the author of a novel, *The Unruly Passions of Eugénie R.*

**Diane DiMassa** is a feminist author and cartoonist. Her works include comics, illustrations, and a graphic novel. She is best known for the character Hothead Paisan, Homicidal Lesbian Terrorist.

**Michael DiMotta** is a freelance illustrator and storyteller, with diverse clients that include DC Comics, Perkins Eastman, Instinct, and Scholastic. Michael has contributed to online daily *Young Bottoms in Love*.

**Mayra Lazara Dole**'s Américas Award Commended Title, *Down to the Bone*, received a starred ALA *Booklist* review, was nominated for ALA Best Books for YA 2009, and made the following lists: *Booklist*'s Top Ten Novels, ALA Rainbow List, and CCBC Top Choices.

**Colman Domingo** is the Tony Award–nominated actor for Best Actor in a Featured Role in a Musical for the critically acclaimed *The Scottsboro Boys*. Colman is the recipient of the OBIE, Lucille Lortel, GLAAD, and Connecticut Critics Circle awards. He has been nominated for the Drama Desk, Drama League, Audelco, and Fred Astaire awards. Colman is the author of *A Boy and His Soul*.

**Larry Duplechan** is the author of five novels, including *Blackbird* (considered the first modern African-American coming-out novel) and the Lambda Literary Award-winning *Got 'Til It's Gone*.

**David Ebershoff** is the author of four books of fiction, including *The Danish Girl*, *The Rose City*, and *Pasadena*. His most recent novel is the international bestseller *The 19th Wife*. Ebershoff has taught creative writing at New York University and Princeton, and currently teaches in the graduate writing program at Columbia University. He is an editor-at-large at Random House and lives in New York City.

As an essayist and reporter, **Paula Gilovich** has contributed to the *New York Times*, *Allure*, and the *Stranger*. Her plays include *Le Roy, Le Roy, Le Roy*; *Water to Breathe*; and *Queertopia*. At About Face Theatre, she worked as a writer and director for the creation of new main-stage and touring plays about the lives and experiences of queer youth.

**Jewelle Gomez** is a writer and activist and the author of the double Lambda Award–winning novel, *The Gilda Stories*. Her fiction, essays, criticism, and poetry have appeared in numerous periodicals. Among them: the *San Francisco Chronicle*, the *New York Times*, the *Advocate*, the *Village Voice*, *Ms. Magazine*, *Essence*, *Callaloo*, and *Black Scholar*.

**Brent Hartinger** is the author of a bunch of books, mostly for teenagers, including *Geography Club* and *Shadow Walkers*. He's won a bunch of awards, including the Lambda (for one of the sequels to *Geography Club*). Also a screenwriter, sometime college instructor, and editor, he helped create AfterElton.com, now one of the largest gay sites on the web and where he still works.

**Adam Haslett** is the author of the short story collection *You Are Not a Stranger Here*, which was a finalist for the Pulitzer Prize and the National Book Award, and the novel *Union Atlantic*, a finalist for the Commonwealth Writers' Prize.

**Randall Keenan** is the author of *A Visitation of Spirits*; *Walking on Water: Black American Lives at the Turn of the Twenty-First Century*; *The Fire This Time*; *Let the Dead Bury Their Dead*. He is associate professor of English and Comparative Literature at UNC-Chapel Hill.

**Lucy Knisley** is an illustrator, comic artist, and author. Her first published book, *French Milk*, is a drawn journal about living (and eating) in Paris with her mother.

**David Leavitt** is the author of the short story collections *Family Dancing* (finalist for the PEN/Faulkner Award and the National Book Critics Circle Award), *A Place I've Never Been*, *The Marble Quilt*, *The Lost Language of Cranes*, *Equal Affections*, *While England Sleeps* (finalist for the *Los Angeles Times* Fiction Prize), *The Page Turner*, *The Body of Jonah Boyd*, and *The Indian Clerk* (finalist for the PEN/Faulkner Award and shortlisted for the IMPAC Dublin award).

**James Lecesne** is an actor, writer, and activist. His Academy Award–winning short film, *Trevor*, inspired the founding of The Trevor Project. In addition to his career as an actor, he has written for TV and he performed several of his own one-man shows, including *Word of Mouth*, which won a New York Drama Desk Award.

**Arthur Levine** is the author of six picture books, including *Monday Is One Day*, illustrated by Julian Hector. He is also the publisher of Arthur A. Levine Books; his list includes works by J. K. Rowling, Shaun Tan, Lisa Yee, Martha Brockenbrough, and David LaRochelle.

**David Levithan** is the author of a whole lot of books, including *Boy Meets Boy*; *The Realm of Possibility*; *Love Is the Higher Law*; *The Lover's Dictionary*; *Nick and Norah's Infinite Playlist* (with Rachel Cohn); and *Will Grayson, Will Grayson* (with John Green).

**Ali Liebegott** is the author of the award-winning books *The Beautifully Worthless* and *The IHOP Papers*. She is currently trying to finish a novel about some Brooklyn misfits and their gambling addictions.

**Malinda Lo** is the author of *Ash* and *Huntress*, two young adult fantasies. *Ash*, a lesbian retelling of Cinderella, was a finalist for the William C. Morris YA Debut Award, the Andre Norton Award for YA Fantasy and Science Fiction, and the Lambda Literary Award. Malinda lives in Northern California with her partner and their dog.

**Gregory Maguire** is the author of many books for children and adults, including the bestselling novel *Wicked*, and was a contributor to *Am I Blue? Coming Out From the Silence*, a collection of short stories for gay and lesbian teenagers. He is a founder and co-director of Children's Literature New England, Incorporated.

**Jaye Maiman** is the author of the Lambda Award-winning Robin Miller Mystery series, now being reissued in beautiful new print and ebook editions by Bella Books (www.bellabooks.com). She lives in Montclair, New Jersey.

**Armistead Maupin** is the author of nine novels, including the six-volume Tales of the City series, *Maybe the Moon*, *The Night Listener*, and, most recently, *Michael Tolliver Lives*.

**Richard McCann** is the author of *Mother of Sorrows*, a work of fiction, and *Ghost Letters*, a collection of poems (1994 Beatrice Hawley Award, 1993 Capricorn Poetry Award). He is also the editor (with Michael Klein) of *Things Shaped in Passing: More "Poets for Life" Writing from the AIDS Pandemic*.

**J. D. McClatchy** is a poet and literary critic. He is editor of the *Yale Review* and president of the American Academy of Arts and Letters.

**Terrence McNally** is the author of many plays, including *LOVE! VALOUR! COMPASSION!* (Tony Award), *Corpus Christi*, *The Lisbon Traviata*, and *Master Class* (Tony Award). For television, he wrote *Andre's Mother* (Emmy Award). His musical theater credits include *Ragtime* and *Kiss of the Spider Woman* (Tony Awards).

**Erika Moen** is a freelance cartoonist with a self-designed degree from Pitzer College in Illustrated Storytelling. She lives in Portland,

Oregon, and is a member of Periscope Studio. She has been happily married to Matthew Nolan since October 2008.

**Sarah Moon** is a teacher, writer, and translator. She lives and works in Brooklyn, New York.

**Martin Moran** lives in New York City where he works as an actor and a writer. He has appeared in many Broadway and Off-Broadway plays including *Titanic, Cabaret, Bells Are Ringing,* and *Floyd Collins*. He won a 2004 OBIE Award for his one-man play, *The Tricky Part*.

**Eileen Myles** was born in Boston and moved to New York in 1974. For her collection of essays, *The Importance of Being Iceland,* she received a Creative Capital/Warhol Foundation grant. *Sorry, Tree* is her most recent book of poems, and her *Inferno* (a poet's novel) is available from OR Books.

**Michael Nava** is the author of the Henry Rios novels and winner of five Lambda Literary Awards and the Bill Whitehead Award for Lifetime Achievement in LGBT literature.

**Jasika Nicole** is primarily an actress, but she is perpetually trying to squeeze in as much drawing and writing in her spare time as her work schedule allows. Nicole has two web comics, *High Yella Magic* and *Closetalkers,* which can be found on her website, jasikanicole.com.

**Eric Orner** is a cartoonist whose works revolve around LGBT issues. He is best known for his acclaimed creation, *The Mostly Unfabulous Social Life of Ethan Green,* which was made into a film in 2005. He has published comic strips and illustrations in the *Washington Post,* the *Boston Globe,* the *San Francisco Chronicle,* and the *New Republic*.

**Erik Orrantia** is a middle school teacher by day and a writer by night. His first published book, *Normal Miguel*, was awarded the Lambda Literary Award for Gay Romance in 2010. He is also the author of *The Equinox Convergence*, and his most recent title, *Taxi Rojo*.

**Julie Anne Peters** has been writing books for young readers for the last 20+ years. Her YA novel *Luna* was a National Book Award finalist and an ALA Best Book for Young Adults. Her other books about gender queer youth include *Keeping You a Secret*; *Far from Xanadu*; *Between Mom and Jo*; *grl2grl: Short Fictions*; *Rage: A Love Story*; and *She Loves You, She Loves You Not . . .* Her most recent title, published in 2010, is *By the Time You Read This, I'll Be Dead*.

**Christopher Rice** published four *New York Times* bestselling novels by the age of thirty and served as a contributing columnist to the *Advocate* magazine for five years. He received a Lambda Literary Award for his second novel, *The Snow Garden*. His criticism and editorials have appeared in the *Washington Post*, *Salon*, and the *Daily Beast*.

**Paul Rudnick**'s plays have been produced both on and off Broadway and around the world. These include *Valhalla*, *The Most Fabulous Story Ever Told*, *I Hate Hamlet*, and *Jeffrey*, for which he won an OBIE, an Outer Critics Circle Award, and the John Gassner Playwriting Award. His novels are *Social Disease* and *I'll Take It*. His screenplays include *Addams Family Values*, the screen adaptation of *Jeffrey*, and *In & Out*.

**Rakesh Satyal** has been published in a variety of anthologies, including the Lambda Award–winning *The Man I Might Become: Gay Men Write about Their Fathers* and the second volume of the Fresh

Men series, which featured an introduction by Andrew Holleran. He is the author of *Blue Boy*.

**Brian Selznick** is a Caldecott-winning author and illustrator of children's books, including *The Invention of Hugo Cabret* and *Wonderstruck*.

**Carter Sickels** is the author of the novel *The Evening Hour*. After spending nearly a decade in New York, Carter left the city to earn a master's degree in folklore at the University of North Carolina at Chapel Hill, and now lives in the Pacific Northwest.

**Susan Stinson** won the Lambda Literary Foundation Outstanding Mid-Career Novelists' Prize for *Fat Girl Dances with Rocks*, *Martha Moody*, and *Venus of Chalk*. She recently completed *Spider in a Tree*, a novel about eighteenth-century Calvinist preacher Jonathan Edwards.

**Lucy Thurber** is the author of eleven plays, including *Where We're Born*, *Scarcity*, and *Monstrosity*. She has been produced by Rattlestick Playwrights Theater and The Atlantic Theater company, among others. She has been commissioned by Playwrights Horizons, Yale Rep, and The Contemporary American Theater Festival. She is a member of New Dramatists and 13P.

A graduate of the MFA in Creative Writing program of the California Institute of the Arts, **Tony Valenzuela** is a longtime community activist and writer whose work has focused on LGBT civil rights, gay men's health, and sexuality. He is currently the Executive Director of the Lambda Literary Foundation.

**Maurice Vellekoop** is the author/illustrator of four books of his own work with Drawn and Quarterly and Green Candy Press. His work has been shown numerous times at the Reactor Gallery in Toronto, the Mayor Gallery in London, and in a traveling group show called "New Pop" that stopped at the Palazzo Fortuny in Venice.

**Linda Villarosa** runs the journalism program at the City College of New York in Harlem. Her novel *Passing for Black* was published in 2008.

**Marc Wolf** is a writer and performer living in New York City. His plays *Another American: Asking and Telling* and *The Road Home: Re-Membering America* have been produced in New York and across the country. He is a recipient of the OBIE Award, GLAAD Award, and two NEA Awards, among others. He stars in the film *Don't Ask, Don't Tell*, adapted from *Another American*.

**Jacqueline Woodson** is the author of a number of award-winning books for children and young adults including *Miracle's Boys*, *The Other Side*, *Show Way*, *Feathers*, *Locomotion*, and *Beneath a Meth Moon*. She lives with her family in Brooklyn, New York.

**Bil Wright** is the author of *Putting Makeup on the Fat Boy*, *When the Black Girl Sings* (a Junior Library Guild selection), and *Sunday You Learn How to Box*, which was a New York Public Library Best Book for the Teen Age. An associate professor of English at the Borough of Manhattan Community College, Bil Wright lives in New York City.

**Doug Wright** is a playwright, librettist, and screenwriter. He received the Pulitzer Prize for Drama in 2004 for his play, *I Am My Own Wife*.

Each one of us deserves a chance to dream for the future, no matter who we love or how we express our gender. The Trevor Project is here for young lesbian, gay, bisexual, transgender, queer, and questioning people to help whenever you or a friend might need to talk to someone. Through our lifesaving programs and information, we work every day to help make the future better for all LGBTQ youth.

The Trevor Project operates the 24-hour Trevor Lifeline, and also TrevorChat online messaging service, both connecting young LGBTQ people to open and accepting counselors, free of charge. Plus, there is TrevorSpace.org, where thousands of young LGBTQ people from all over the world can connect in a safe and accepting social space. Trevor is also on Facebook, Twitter, and YouTube, connecting young people with positive messages every day.

If you or someone you care about feels depressed or is considering taking their own life, please call The Trevor Lifeline at: 866-488-7386. The call is free and confidential.

Visit www.TheTrevorProject.org to learn more.

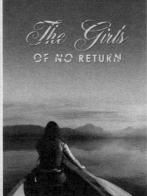